# Down Into This Land

Selected Poetry of Edgar Lee Masters

Chosen, Edited, and with an Introduction by
Ryan Guth

TRANSCENDENT ZERO PRESS
HOUSTON, TEXAS
2022

Copyright © Transcendent Zero Press, 2022.

Introduction copyright © Ryan Guth, 2022.

ISBN:978-1-946460-34-9

Library of Congress Control Number: 2021947363

No portion of this book may be reprinted without written consent from the editor Ryan Guth, or the publisher Transcendent Zero Press except for brief citations in reviews or scholarly articles.

To contact the publisher: Editor@transcendentzeropress.org.

Cover design by Akeem Abdul Olawuyi

Photo of Ryan Guth by John McCommon

Photo of Edgar Lee Masters in public domain

Cover photo of Starved Rock State Park, Illinois in public domain taken from *goodfreephotos.com*.

Published by Transcendent Zero Press

Houston, Texas

*www.transcendentzeropress.org*

FIRST EDITION

# Down Into This Land

Selected Poetry of Edgar Lee Masters

Chosen, Edited, and with an Introduction by
Ryan Guth

Reprint editions of books by Edgar Lee Masters:

*Across Spoon River* (with an introduction by Ronald Primeau)
*The Sangamon* (with an introduction by Charles E. Burgess)
*Spoon River Anthology* (edited, introduced, and annotated by John E. Hallwas)

ଓଃ

Other books by Ryan Guth:

*Body and Soul*
*Home Truths*

## CONTENTS

Acknowledgements / xi
The Poetry of Edgar Lee Masters / xiii
A Note on the Text / xxviii

from ***A Book of Verses*** (1898)

    Lines Written in the Desplaines Forest / 3
    Byron / 5
    Ballade of Salem Town / 6

from ***The Blood of the Prophets*** (1905)

    Ballad of the Traitor's Soul / 9
    Epitaph for a Dead Senator / 11

from ***Songs and Sonnets*** (1910)

    Love's Philosophy / 15
    Eternal Woman / 17

from ***Songs and Sonnets, 2nd Series*** (1912)

    Past and Present / 21
    The World Spirit / 22

from ***Songs and Satires*** (1916)

    Silence / 25
    The Sign / 27
    In the Cage / 28

from ***The Great Valley*** (1916)

    The Mourner's Bench / 33
    The Gospel of Mark / 35

from ***Toward the Gulf*** (1918)

    Tomorrow is my Birthday / 43

from ***Starved Rock*** (1919)

    Starved Rock / 55
    Wild Birds / 58
    Oh You Sabbatarians! / 59
    Thyamis / 61
    I Shall Go Down into this Land / 63
    The House on the Hill / 65

from ***The Open Sea*** (1921)

    Ulysses / 69

from ***The New Spoon River*** (1924)

    Marx the Sign Painter / 77
    Yet Sing Low / 78
    Henry Zoll the Miller / 79
    The Tombs of the Governors / 80
    Frank Blatt / 82
    Mrs. Frank Blatt / 83
    Horace Knight / 84
    Joseph Ruhe / 85
    Roland Farley / 86
    Jack Kelso / 87
    Conrad Herron / 88
    Thomas Nelson / 89

from ***Selected Poems*** (1925)

    The Corn / 93
    Worlds / 99

from ***Lichee Nuts*** (1930)

    On Contentment / 105
    Yet Wei at the Thalia Theatre / 106
    Full Moon on the Bowery / 107
    Saving Tears / 108
    Origin of Sin / 109
    The Death of Hip Lung / 110
    The Departure of Yet Wei / 111
    Yet Wei's Poem / 112

from ***Invisible Landscapes*** (1935)

    Invocation / 115
    Invisible Landscapes / 117
    Hymn to the Earth / 121
    The God of the Ailanthus / 130
    Hoboken from 23rd Street / 132
    Gettysburg / 134

from ***Poems of People*** (1936)

    Thothmes: Central Park and The Drive / 137
    Weekend by the Sea / 139
    The Red Cross Nurse / 141
    The Grandson / 143

from ***More People*** (1939)

    Old Georgie Kirby / 147
    Nathaniel Page / 149
    Quack-Grass / 150
    Lands End / 152

from ***Illinois Poems*** (1941)

    Near Fourth Bridge / 157
    Havana, Illinois / 159
    Wild Geese / 162

from ***Along the Illinois*** (1942)

    The Prairie: Sandridge / 165
    Invulnerable Earth / 167
    Prairie Wind / 168
    Spring Lake Village / 172

from ***The Harmony of Deeper Music*** (1976)

    Voice of the Valley / 177
    The Sleepers / 178
    At Midnight in Mytilene / 179
    Medusa / 183
    There is Labor Whither Thou Goest / 185
    In Memory of Alexander Dexter Masters / 186
    *from* Vignettes from Vermont
        II. Charley the Hermit / 187
        III. Old Mrs. Comstock / 188
        IV. Ruby Deems / 189
    Planting Trees at Tor House / 190
    Not to See Sandridge Again / 191
    The Hills of Big Creek / 192
    A New Day Dawns / 195

***Uncollected and Unpublished Poems*** (1918-1944)

    Spoon River Revisited / 199
    I Am America / 203
    Clarence Darrow / 205
    The Return / 208
    Hymn to the Unknown God / 215
    End of August / 219
    Li Po / 221

Amphimixis / 223
Hymn to the Universes / 226
On Seeing *Tannhäuser* / 229
The Triumph of Earth / 230
The Lotus in Illinois / 237
The Bridge / 239
This Bloody Age / 240
An Illinois Scene / 241
The Poet's Immortal Fame / 242
Two Sonnets / 243

**"Pieces by Puckett":**
*a sampling of Masters' comic and erotic light verse*

To an Orphan Clam / 247
Compensation / 249
Let the Lower Lights be Burning / 250
Two Limericks / 252
Heavenly Dispensation / 253
Nature / 254

Notes to the Poems / 259

# ACKNOWLEDGEMENTS

Grateful acknowledgement is made first of all to John D. C. Masters and the late Hilary Masters, for their generous permission to reprint all poetry by Edgar Lee Masters still under copyright.

Secondly to Dr. Alison Rieke, who gave freely of her time, expertise, and assistance at the beginning of this project, when I was a doctoral student at the University of Cincinnati many years ago.

Thirdly to three wonderful librarians, for invaluable guidance in navigating their collections remotely and arranging for pdf's of selected Masters manuscripts: Paul Civitelli, Library Assistant at the Beinecke Rare Book and Manuscript Library; Christopher Schnell, Manuscript Curator, and Michelle Miller, Manuscripts Librarian, both at the Abraham Lincoln Presidential Library and Museum.

Fourthly to the following, for their contributions of information and advice: Spencer Guth and Mari Tanaka elucidated many of Masters' allusions to aspects of Asian culture. Spencer also provided valuable insights into classical Greek and Roman history, the American Civil War, and World Wars I and II. Brendan Rowe and Tony Rafalowski assisted with the Biblical references in "Ballad of the Traitor's Soul." Alex Aitken, Nicholas Ashbaugh, John Koons, and Elizabeth Weston helped to clarify Masters' mycological terminology in the poem "Amphimixis." Steven Wood assisted with etymologies and alternate spellings of some of Masters' delightful lexical oddities. Elizabeth Weston and Elizabeth Ford Guth read a draft of the "Introduction" and provided much-needed commentary.

Lastly:

To Dr. John Hallwas, for permission to cite material from *The Vision of This Land* (1976).

To the University of Texas Press, for permission to cite material from Ronald Primeau's *Beyond Spoon River: The Legacy of Edgar Lee Masters* (1981).

To the University of Illinois Press, for permission to cite material from Herbert K. Russell's *Edgar Lee Masters: A Biography* (2001).

Texts for the poems "On Seeing *Tannhäuser*" and "The Triumph of Earth" were provided by the Beinecke Rare Book and Manuscript Library, Yale University.

Texts for the following poems were provided by the Abraham Lincoln Presidential Library and Museum: "An Illinois Scene," "This Bloody Age," "Two Sonnets," "To an Orphan Clam," "Compensation," "Let the Lower Lights be Burning," "Two Limericks," "Heavenly Dispensation," and "Nature."

THE POETRY OF EDGAR LEE MASTERS:
Toward a Reappraisal

The aims of the present volume are simple: first and foremost to bring together, for the general reader, a book's worth of the best shorter poems by Edgar Lee Masters. A century ago, he was one of America's most well-known and widely published writers, yet today less than half a dozen of his more than 50 volumes of verse, fiction, essays, biography, and regional history are in print, and only one of them has secured a permanent place in our literature. That one, *Spoon River Anthology*, is of course so firmly established and so easily available that I have omitted it from consideration for this book. But every other collection of poems published by Masters from 1898 to 1942 is represented here, along with *The Harmony of Deeper Music* (a posthumous 1976 publication, exquisitely chosen by Frank K. Robinson from an archive of Masters manuscripts in the Humanities Research Center at the University of Texas, Austin). I have also included a number of poems which appeared only in magazines and newspapers of the day, or as privately-printed broadsides circulated among a few friends. Finally, a small sampling of other poems in manuscript (from collections in Yale University's Beinecke Rare Book and Manuscript Library, and the Abraham Lincoln Presidential Library) here make their debut in print.

As far as I am aware, then, this book is the first "Selected Poems" to appear since Masters' own in 1925; thus it is the only publication to date which can claim to represent the author's entire five-decade career as a working poet. There is Herbert Russell's 1991 volume, *The Enduring River: Edgar Lee Masters' Uncollected Spoon River Poems*, but that slender volume merely reprints a few pieces specifically chosen for their association with Masters' most famous work. Thus, Russell's selection—good as it is—serves only to reinforce the entrenched misconception that Masters wrote nothing of lasting value outside the context of the *Anthology*.

Refuting that misconception is of course my other purpose in offering these poems to the public. Masters himself, it must be acknowledged, is partly to blame for the bedraggled state of his literary reputation. As his biographer Herbert Russell reports, in the ten years following *Spoon River*'s initial publication in 1915—pressed for funds in the face of a lengthy, fractious, and embarrassingly well-publicized divorce—he produced no fewer than thirteen new books (Russell, *Edgar Lee Masters* 123; hereafter

"*ELM*"). Six of these were volumes of "new" miscellaneous verse, hastily assembled and frequently padded with inferior material from the four collections he had put out before *Spoon River* (three of them under his own vanity publishing imprint, The Rooks Press). As an example of Masters' rush to publish, Russell calculates that the entire contents of 1918's *Toward the Gulf* were written and arranged in a mere five weeks (*ELM* 170).

Even in his last creative decade, during which he virtually remade himself as a writer, Masters' increasingly eccentric, self-destructive behavior toward his prestigious New York publishers, Macmillan, Liveright, and Dodd Mead, did nothing to ameliorate his dimming visibility in the East Coast literary world (*ELM* 299, 338). Eventually, after years of squabbling over advances, royalties, loans, and advertising, he abruptly abandoned commercial publishers altogether in favor of a small regional press, James A. Decker of Prairie City, Illinois. Decker printed Masters' last two verse collections (*Illinois Poems* and *Along the Illinois*) in limited editions of 500 and 340 copies respectively (*ELM* 339, 345). Thus, although the latter volume in particular contained some of the finest poetry Masters would ever write, the very obscurity of its publication ensured that the most influential reviewers paid scant attention to it (Flanagan 141-142).

The problem of Masters' reputation is more complex than that, however. Ironically, the single greatest obstacle he faced in his literary career may well have been the sudden and astounding success of *Spoon River Anthology* itself. It is almost worth speculating (as Masters himself did) whether his subsequent literary standing might not be higher if he had never written his best-known book. "*Spoon River* has always been in my way," he groused to his friend Arthur Davison Ficke in 1935. "And yet I think every book I wrote since then had pieces in it as good or better than anything in *Spoon River*" (qtd. in *ELM* 303).

Some context will illustrate the accuracy of Masters' complaint. *Spoon River* made its first book appearance in 1915, in the midst of a bumpy transition from the so-called "Genteel Tradition" in American letters (mostly pale imitators of Walt Whitman's better-behaved contemporaries Longfellow and Whittier), to the first generation of assertive, self-aware Modernists, who were publishing and reviewing in such taste-making journals as *Poetry* and *The Dial*. Eager, no doubt, to shake off the "Genteel" poets' vague idealizations of "Truth" and "Beauty," many in the Modernist camp were quick to lionize Masters for his exposure of untidy sexual hankerings and Macchiavellian political/financial maneuverings, as they played out in his small midwestern town (Flanagan 25-31). No less a figure than Ezra Pound, writing in *The Egoist*, praised Masters unequivocally: "AT LAST!," he famously proclaimed, "at last America has discovered a poet!" (qtd. in Flanagan 27). Such high (and highly-placed) praise unfortunately contributed to an expectation that Masters would go on to align himself with the emerging avant-garde of Pound and T.S. Eliot. When his subsequent work failed to satisfy this expectation, forward-looking critics and anthologists like Louis Untermeyer would eventually declare, and could themselves believe, that "with *Spoon River Anthology* Masters arrived, and left." (qtd. in Flanagan 34).

   The truth is that Masters stands somewhat apart from both the Genteel and the Modernist strands of American poetry. Like Shelley, Emerson, and Walt Whitman, the writers who most influenced his thought and art, Masters conceived of the poet's role as essentially a public one: that of a conscientious, critically-minded citizen who sought, through the written word, to address his or her countrymen directly and honestly regarding issues of importance to their shared civilization. "When it speaks for a land and celebrates a tribe," he wrote in his 1937 study of Whitman, "it has done the greatest work that poetry can do" (Masters, *Whitman* 307). Such a project stands diametrically opposed to the hermetically inclined Modernists—and it is that public orientation, I suspect, that finally made Masters so indigestible to them. For most of the age in which Masters lived, the ascendant New Critics asserted that the literary text was entirely self-sufficient, requiring nothing external to it in order to manifest its meaning: neither from the writer's intentions nor the reader's, nor from any values or assumptions they might share. Yet those very assumptions—and the consciously rhetorical, persuasive stances adopted by a writer to invoke them—are of central importance to Masters' poetry, especially in the decade or so after *Spoon River* was published. To ignore that fact is to misread him. Thus, as Ronald Primeau puts it in his provocatively titled study *Beyond Spoon River*, "[f]rom the start, Masters' reputation was built on the wrong foundation" (95). What follows, then, is my own attempt to provide a new foundation, a new basis for understanding and assessing Masters' achievement as a lyric poet.

≈

The period 1915-1925 is the most problematic in Masters' career. While poems like "I Shall Go Down Into This Land" or "The Corn" reflect something of Whitman's great-hearted optimism and openness to experience, Masters' own "yawp" tends to be far more "barbaric—or at least barbed— than his mentor's, his attitude toward his culture and its beliefs far more negative and critical.

"In the Cage," from his 1916 volume *Songs and Satires,* provides as good an example of this as any, and remains a remarkably forward-looking commentary on sex and gender roles. Less a dramatic monologue than an interior one, the poem records a male speaker's shifting perceptions of a woman ("you") with whom he has just spent the night in a Chicago hotel room: specifically a shift away from his complacent reliance on conventional stereotypes of "the being feminine," and her place in extramarital sexual relationships, toward a substantial critique of those very stereotypes. At first, certain of being the possessor of his mistress both physically and emotionally, he sees her as "fully under my heart's sway... a weak thing for a strong man's play." Even the rhyme here is apt, calling our attention to shopworn phrases like "heart's sway," which are as un-original as the attitudes and behaviors they ascribe to the pair and their relationship.

But as his lover prepares to leave, the speaker's observations soon jar with his off-the-rack assumptions about her "weakness":

> I know our partings. You will faintly smile
> And look at me with eyes that have no guile,
> Or have too much, and pass into the sphere
> Where you keep independent life meanwhile.
> How do you live without me, is the fear?

Precisely *whose* fear is expressed in that question is not obvious at first. If hers, as we are likely to assume at first, then the question is merely another presumptuous assertion of his "sway" over her, his belief that he can know what she is thinking. The next two lines, however, strongly imply that the "fear" is actually his own: "You do not lean upon me, ask my love, or wonder / Of other loves I may have hidden...." Clearly, it is *his* anticipation of *her* departure—not only from their love-nest, but from the expected script which calls for clinging and jealousy from her—which spurs his own increasingly uneasy realizations. Thus his question is the pivot upon which the entire poem turns, from unthinking certainty to probing doubt about the untested assumptions he has relied on up to this point.

Yet the speaker's doubt is more than just a rejection of his previous complacency. As we read on, we see him thinking the problem through to its deeper source: the failure of "all that has been preached or sung or spoken / Of woman's tragedy in woman's fall" to account for the behavior of the real woman in front of him. Having had that realization, he is better able to understand what is actually occurring:

> there you stand,
> Your heart and life as firmly in command
> Of your resolve as mine is… you have cast
> Veil after veil of ideals or pretense
> With which men clothe the being feminine
> To satisfy their lordship, or their sense
> Of ownership…making comical
> The poems and the tales of woman's fall….

As a poem authored by Edgar Lee Masters, "In the Cage" is itself a reply to those older "poems and tales": a refusal to recognize the authority granted by tradition to such received cultural "wisdom"—which is, and may always have been, inadequate to the lived experience of men and women. Of course this cultural dialogue is largely implicit in the poem, subordinate to our interest in the speaker and his honest, if fumbling, attempts to re-evaluate his uncritical acceptance of conventional belief. Masters' realism is all the more impressive in that his speaker's tentative gains in perception begin all too soon to waver: as soon as his lover has left, he imagines that "life himself will track / Your wanderings and bring you back…." Apparently projecting his own masculinity onto all of existence ("life himself"), he fantasizes an ultimate victory over any impulse of her own to remain "independent" of him. And yet that fantasy brings him no pleasure, no sense of triumph or restored "sway" over her. Having once seen through the falsehoods of "all that has been preached or sung or spoken…" he is forced to predict the more likely mixture of "love and hatred and… silent rage" which would "cage" them as soon as they are reunited.

"In the Cage" gives us the intermediary of a fictionalized speaker and situation: it is a solid, well-constructed dramatic monologue, something we have a name for and know how to engage with as readers. But in his work of the 1910's and '20's, Masters' public address is frequently much more direct and accusatory, as in the once-notorious "Oh You Sabbatarians" from *Starved Rock* (1919). Although I have my own grave doubts about its artistic integrity, this piece certainly challenges the understood writer-reader relationship, and illustrates the extremes to which the poet was willing to go in his poetry of cultural dialogue.

Immediately noticeable in "Oh You Sabbatarians" is Masters' construction, not of a specified *speaker*, but a specified *audience*: the grossly caricatured "sabbatarians, methodists and puritans" in line 1 (even my

21st-century spell-checker had to be talked out of treating all three with the Capital-Letter respect the poet has denied them!). These "chaste and epicene spirits," with their conventional proprieties, their "dull assemblies, / Charades, cantatas, and lectures," are ranged against "we, the free spirits… Drinkers of the wine made by Jesus, / Worshipers of fire and of God, / Who made the grape…." This reduction to cartoonish extremes of dutifully pious teetotalers and sensual, unpredictable "free spirits," along with its too-obvious reversal of the Sacred and the Profane (at least as polite Chicago or Spring Lake society has agreed to understand them), soon begins to feel like so much adolescent rebellion.

Yet in the context of Masters' Whitmanesque poetics of public address, these extreme rhetorical tactics might be more than just an aesthetic misstep. The poem's "you"—the church-going, business-owning members of polite society—might very well have admitted, if pressed, that their "civic meetings," "teas," and "receptions" were in fact less important for their own sake than as opportunities to see or be seen. The dissemination of art and ideas really was, for the majority of such attendees, a mask (or masque?) for social climbing or "work[ing] up business." Masters may, as they say, have a point there.

But even if we grant him that point, surely the poem's gross exaggerations ("eyes blind to colors, / Ears deaf to sound, / Fingers insensitive"), and jeering ridicule ("your young men of clammy hands / And fetid breath"), simply go too far. Most readers, I imagine, would accept Herbert Russell's dismissal of the poem as simply a petty "revenge" exacted on specific but unnamed individuals whose disapproval of the poet's own free-thinking, free-loving (read: adulterous) lifestyle had hounded him out of a long-hoped-for writing retreat in socially conservative lakeside Michigan (Russell, "After" 79-80). By stuffing a poem with such over-the-top personal spleen, then including that poem in a book and publishing it with no less an entity than The Macmillan Company of New York, Masters has broken the most basic rules of decency, artistic or otherwise; after all, none of his intended targets would have had access to a similar forum for response. The poet is a bully, abusing both them and his art.

I wonder, though, if such reactions on our part—those feelings of annoyance, even embarrassment, at Masters' flouting of all pretense to artistic decorum—might be exactly what he intended to evoke. If his purpose is in fact to ridicule conventional *salon* behavior, then his own flagrant violation of unspoken aesthetic proprieties may simply be another expression of that ridicule. The poem's very existence in print forces us to realize that there are in fact no natural laws governing poetic discourse. We can choose to respond as our own socialization would prompt us…

or we could, possibly, begin to rethink for ourselves what is legitimately "artistic" and what is not.

Perhaps Masters himself, in another passage from his book on Whitman, has provided some justification for his own unruly behavior in print:

> It is not strange that Whitman had no sons dedicated to carrying on his work. It is logical, however, that he had sons bent on avenging the ruin of the America to which Whitman gave his life. These by their satire and anathema bewail and curse the state to which the republic and the people were reduced by deliberate executions against the last hope of liberty in this world, as Jefferson called the United States. (*Whitman* 309)

"Satire" and "anathema," of course, are explicitly public in nature: that is, they are responses to real, material circumstances. They are precisely *not*, in other words, the kind of autonomous, self-justifying utterances favored by the reigning High Modernist writers and New Critics of Masters' literary maturity.

Interestingly, Masters' "sabbatarians"—with their connections to law, church, and business, their capacity for self-restraint (sexually, if not materialistically), and their implacable enmity toward the "viewers of life as Freedom and Beauty"—begin to sound a great deal like another one of Masters' creations: Deacon Thomas Rhodes, the central villain of *Spoon River Anthology*. As it happens, Rhodes's own epitaph-poem employs the exact rhetorical technique used a few years later by the speaker of "Oh You Sabbatarians": that is, he constructs and then addresses a highly specific audience of his perceived enemies: "you liberals... You sailors through heights imaginative, / Blown about by erratic currents, tumbling into air pockets...." These "sailors" could easily be the same "free spirits" from the later poem, "Flourish[ing] on the hills of variable winds." Perhaps it is the Rhodeses of the world—not its "free spirits"—who have divided the world into a simplistic "you" versus "we," those "seekers of earth's treasures" who are "self-contained, compact, harmonized, / Even to the end." And if Rhodes's claims to completeness, consistency, and rationality represent Masters' vision of a culture ruled by "the Bible and the Banks" (as he put it in his 1937 Whitman biography), then his scorn for that culture in "Oh You Sabbatarians"—with all of its obvious bias and transgressive behavior—may simply be a way of stepping outside that culture's impenetrable self-justification. How much distance is there, really, between Masters' poem and Allen Ginsberg's "Howl"?

By the end of the 1920's, Masters had largely moved on (or cooled off) from this mode of public address and explicit social commentary. In this late period of his work, one can identify three major strands: a more abstract poetry of spiritual and philosophical speculation; a number of portraits and character pieces which seem to take up where *Spoon River* left off; and an ambitious new emphasis on what we might think of as the spirit of place.

In such discursive pieces as "Hymn to the Universes" and "The Triumph of Earth," Masters combines the optimism of Whitman with the pessimism of Shelley, adventurously examining the moral nature of humankind, even our place within the vastness of creation. "Hymn to the Universes," for example, concludes with a triumphant claim for the significance of humanity on the cosmic stage:

> I will sing the spirit of man
> Which, whether it emerged from earth and rocks
> Or was separately created, is the transcendent miracle,
> And may fitly face the universes as an equal,
> And eye them with satire,
> Wisdom, and solemn music.

Yet this claim to "equal" stature does not absolve mankind from critical appraisal. In the slightly later "Triumph of Earth,"

> we are told by a man-god
> To love one another, but the Supreme God made us
> So that we cannot love one another....
> Even imagination, which can heal, can lift,
> Has an equal capacity to wound, to destroy;
> And is used in age after age over the earth to wound, to
>     destroy....

As if in humanity's defense, however, later passages in the same poem declare that "Nothing in the earth is gauged ideally to man," whose heart "aches because the earth defrauds and deceives," and "because the will must ever be asserted... or surrendered, and that is death." Even so, the final "triumph" is ours, not Earth's: the greatest force, the greatest good Masters can find in his far-flung survey of material creation, is the peculiarly human capacity to perceive ideals and moral foundations that are not clearly manifest in our physical surroundings:

> For hate cannot wholly destroy our love;
> Fear and doubt cannot wholly destroy our belief.
> As there is rock below the quicksands and the swamps,
> Beneath the absurdity of this our earth-life
> We feel the rock of eternal truth....

∽

Concurrent with these brooding philosophical meditations, the later "poems of people" appear to continue *Spoon River*'s focus on the forces that shape individual lives, although with some significant differences in technique and method. With a few exceptions ("Old Georgie Kirby" and "Nathaniel Page" from the 1939 book *More People*), the individuals depicted are not yet dead—or, to be more accurate, their current state of existence is not at issue. In addition, the majority of these poems employ a third-person perspective rather than *Spoon River*'s blunt first-person testimony. The poems tend to be longer as well, their situations more developed than a brief epitaph poem could reasonably accommodate: "The Red Cross Nurse," for example, is almost a short story in verse, while "The Grandson" packs a novel's worth of event into its 56 lines.

Even more striking (and surprising, if one comes to them after the vehemence and personal spleen of the earlier "public" poems) is a new reticence on Masters' part: a willingness to withhold explicit authorial comment in favor of evocative situations that are allowed to resonate in the reader's own mind. For instance, Masters' Red Cross Nurse (from *Poems of People*, 1936), is actually an out-of-work actress named Helen Vandegrift, a woman with an abortion in her recent past. We also learn that her partner left her, to go to war ("he said")... and with that, he disappears from the poem. Those details stay in the backs of our minds, though, as we read about the artist Aiken's war poster: depicted as a nurse tending a wounded soldier, Helen is transformed into a motherly symbol of comfort and caring for the frightened boys who will carry it with them into the strange new noise and gloom of World War I trenches and aerial bombardments. Is it possible that her ex-lover, on his own tour of duty, might someday see that poster—or that, seeing it, he would recognize her? And supposing he did, would he be reminded of the abortion? Or would he even have known about it? And what about Helen: will she feel a sense of accomplishment by becoming a part of the war effort—or will the completed image on Aiken's easel bring back her own traumatic memories of those back-alley "surgeons and a night of horror, / Grappling with death," herself "attended by a nurse"? The poem provokes such questions, but makes it impossible even to guess at any answers.

If "The Red Cross Nurse" stirs us to curiosity about the circumstances it has set in motion for its characters, "The Grandson" (also from *Poems of People*) poses questions of its own directly to the reader. The prime mover in this complex, shifting web of sexual and familial relationships is the male character Perkins, who has "stray[ed]" from his wife "to Captain Tanner's daughter, Valeria." Refusing any easy set of punishments or rewards, Masters instead allows the simple realities of infidelity, divorce, and re-marriage to play out, eventually producing a baby boy—Theodore—whose very existence brings his grandfather, the lonely Captain, back into nourishing human contact… while necessarily, of course, condemning Perkins' first wife to "unhappiness / For her true heart." But does the innocent Captain not have "A right to happiness, though you prove / That Perkins and Valeria should waive / Their hope, give up their guilty love?" Furthermore,

> Though we scorn
> Perkins as a man forsworn,
> How else had Theodore been born?
> Suppose he means much to his kind
> As statesman, thinker, or a mind!
> If not, just leave out man and wife:
> Did Theodore have the right to life?

These may sound like rhetorical questions, but the implied answers are not so easy to determine, which is of course the poem's point: there is no solution that delivers the justice or happiness each character deserves.

Masters' 1930 collection, *Lichee Nuts*, provides another variation on the *Spoon River* method. As with the miscellaneous collections *Poems of People* and *More People*, there is a mixture of first-person and third-person narration within the collection, and the characters depicted are still very much alive. Like *Spoon River*, though, *Lichee Nuts* is focused on the inhabitants of a single place, an urban one this time: New York City's Chinatown community.

Here, before continuing, I need to acknowledge what I expect will be the most objectionable feature of this material: that is, Masters' reliance on stereotyped Chinese-American speech as a unifying style for his book. I make no excuses for him on this point: he was more than capable of hearing and accurately rendering a variety of speech idioms, and he should have done so in *Lichee Nuts*. And yet there is much in this material which reflects not only Masters' considerable knowledge of Asian culture, but a profound sympathy with the sadness peculiar to geographic and cultural dislocation.

Take the delightfully titled "Full Moon on the Bowery," for example. Even a casual reading of this poem reveals the aching homesickness of its main character, Harry Chin, as he compares the sight of the moon among New York tenements and skyscrapers with night-memories of his homeland. But his real emotions are far more complex than that, expressed in a layer of oddly specific allusions which, when identified, allow us to see into the depths of Harry's mind and heart. To him, that full moon

> looked like a wilted Nelumbian Lotus
> In the hands of Hua Hsien,
> The goddess of flowers, when she stands
> By the shore of Hangchou.

"Nelumbian Lotus," it turns out, is a particular species of water-lily native only to North America... *not* to Asia. Thus, the "wilted" flower Harry imagines the deity holding, as she stands by the Hangchou shore, is more than just a simile suggesting that the familiar moon looks out of sorts in its unfamiliar setting. Precisely because Harry has placed his Taoist goddess and her uprooted American lotus in a specific *Chinese* location, the simile becomes a mirror of his own cultural displacement, as an Asian immigrant living in that most American of metropoli. Even Hangchou, a bayside city on the Pacific, could reflect a parallel with coastal New York City. Perhaps, in his unconscious mind, Harry believes—or hopes—that the wilted lotus (now a symbol for his homesick self as well as a simile for the moon he is gazing at) will be revived by the goddess's touch. There is a consoling beauty in Harry's concluding recollection of

> the night wind over Hangchou,
> Which heaps the spun glass of sea foam
> Against the reeds with the sound of blown frost
> Where the naked moon bathes alone
> With streaming hair.

And yet, and yet... is that "naked moon" finally back where she belongs, in familiar country? Or is she now merely "alone," even on the Hangchou shore? Has Harry's homesickness colored even that cherished memory?

Such delicate insights as these coexist uneasily with the thoughtless use of cartoon "Chinaman" talk in many of the other poems.

❧

To my mind, the most important work of Masters' last creative decade is his ambitious exploration of the spirit of place. As with the character pieces, this is less a brand-new phenomenon than the late blooming of another career-long preoccupation. After all, depictions of the beloved woodlands and prairies of his Illinois childhood go back as far as the "Lines Written in the Desplaines Forest," from *A Book of Verses* (1898). However, his late renderings of these and other landscapes are far more than mere regionalism or derivative Romanticism. Demonstrating an increasingly contemplative, at times mystical, sensibility, Masters—like Wordsworth before him—intuits a living, sometimes sentient, "spirit in the woods." But he explores that spirit more deeply than Wordsworth did, ascribing personality, even specific emotions, to the places he contemplates. There are glimpses of this growing preoccupation at least as far back as *The New Spoon River* (1924), whose "Joseph Ruhe" speaks of the dead who are now able to understand "the sorrow of hills" that the living cannot perceive. But it is not until his 1935 collection, *Invisible Landscapes*, that he finds the name for this theme and the expressive means to do it full justice. Once achieved, however, the "invisible landscape" will be incorporated into every one of Masters' subsequent collections, including the posthumously published *Harmony of Deeper Music* (1976).

The best of these poems are a compound of memory and observation, as in the title poem from *Invisible Landscapes*, where the speaker seems to immerse himself simultaneously within an actual and a remembered scene:

> When over Starved Rock you watch
> The crows at evening fly,
> Within your heart to match
> Is a sky for that lonely sky.
> Your longings, aches, and dreams
> Come from the landscape's scar,
> Where soldiers by these streams
> Went hasting forth to war
> And never returned again,
> Except as leaves that fell
> To feed the landscape's pain....

This is the richest vein of poetic ore Masters ever mined, at once evocative and enigmatic. Does that "pain" arise from the landscape itself, or from the viewer's own "aches"? Or is it some residue of emotion left there by those long-ago soldiers, tramping a "scar" into the place on their way to battlefields from which they hoped to return?

In "The Prairie: Sandridge," seven years later (from the 1942 collection *Along the Illinois*), the poet suggests his own answers to some of these questions: "the spirit of the scene," that "presence" which one can learn to sense in the landscape, is "not wholly nature, and not man, / But made of these, made even of the dead / Whose living hands reaped here...." Thus all three, as we might have expected—the place itself, the lingering memory of its former inhabitants, and the observer in the present—contribute to that multi-layered "invisible landscape." Typical of all these experiences is the speaker who beholds, or remembers, a well-known place and the people who inhabited it, then records a moment of rapt, self-dissolving identification with it and/or them.

From *Invisible Landscapes* to the end of Masters' creative life, remembered places more and more come to replace the actual ones, yet his minutely inspected responses to them remain clear and undeceived. In "Not to See Sandridge Again" (published posthumously in *The Harmony of Deeper Music*), the poet's inventory of what has "vanished" from the scenes of his childhood seems to make him more aware of, or anxious about, the invisible landscape's mutability. "Earth even may change, but if the love it stirs / Remains, is Earth then changed?" To address this question, Masters examines the phenomenon of memory itself:

> If man must pass... if harvesters
> Themselves are gathered, and old men sink like grass
> Into the quiet of the universe,
> Yet memory keeps them, they are never less.

And that remembering, he concludes, "is eternal life for them, for me." But memory itself is fragile, susceptible to distortion from the conflicts in sensory input caused by the bald facts of death and change. And if memory is so ephemeral, what about the invisible landscapes that partly reside there? Perhaps, then,

> If gazing on a dead face is to blot
> What the dead was in life, so not to see
> Sandridge again may be the better lot.

A bittersweet conclusion to the last and greatest theme of Masters' career.

❧

Following the selections from individual volumes and from Masters' uncollected and unpublished work, I have added a brief section titled *Pieces by Puckett*. The title is Masters' own, and appears on the typescript pages of all six of the poems I have included to represent this lighter side of the poet's work: the occasional comic and erotic poems, written for his own amusement and sometimes shared with friends.

According to Masters scholar John E. Hallwas, the pseudonym "Lute Puckett" has a complex history, ultimately connected with the ageing rake "Lucius Atherton" from *Spoon River Anthology*. In his later years, Masters enjoyed writing the occasional obscene letter, in Atherton's voice, to his hometown friend Edwin Reese. When "Lucius," or "Lewd," felt like adding a poem to the letter, the pseudonym was changed to "Lute Puckett" (Hallwas 77). This name does not appear in *Spoon River*, although there is a "Lydia Puckett" whose boyfriend caught her with Atherton (raising the interesting possibility that Masters imagined Lute to be a natural child of Atherton with Lydia, born and raised out of wedlock). Atherton's poem in *Spoon River* is essentially a lament for the effects of age on his sexual appeal and performance, which left him, by the end, a "[t]oothless, discarded, rural Don Juan." Perhaps, then, these "Pieces by Puckett" allowed Masters—sex-obsessed to the end of his own life—a bit of a laugh at his own expense. In that light I have included these pieces, which as far as I know the poet never intended for publication.

❧

In both his writing and his reading, Edgar Lee Masters characteristically valued the thought itself more highly than its particular expression. Introducing a volume of Emerson's essays, the poet (then in his seventies) argued passionately for the superiority of Goethe's *Faust* to "anything that Shakespeare wrote," because "*Faust* is the story of a soul that struggled through the welter of life to a spiritual victory, while Hamlet died in a duel and Macbeth lamented tomorrow, tomorrow and tomorrow" (Masters, *Living Thoughts* 36). Just so, the Emerson presented to us by Masters, in his own selection from the philosopher's work, cares not at all if a writer "trips and stammers," so long as his "message" can "find method and imagery, articulation and melody. Though it were dumb, it would speak. If not—if there be no such God's word in the man—what care we how adroit, how fluent, how brilliant he is?" (qtd. in *Living Thoughts* 111).

Such a statement could easily be Masters' own. By turns compassionate, exasperated, tender, dismissive, sometimes self-pitying, sometimes ecstatic, sometimes frankly sentimental—and on occasion hilariously pornographic—he is never more nor less than himself, even when hiding behind a self-puncturing pseudonym. Such emotional candor, however cranky or apoplectic it may get, guarantees his most visionary utterances as well, with all their "wonder at the fate of the human heart that can burn with such longings and such dreams and still have no power either in itself or in the circumstances of life to realize them" (Masters, *Across* 406).

# A NOTE ON THE TEXT

As stated above, all of Edgar Lee Masters' published collections of poetry are represented here—except, of course, for *Spoon River Anthology*, which is still easily available, and in any event is best read as a single book-length work. The same could possibly be said of its sequel, *The New Spoon River*, but since that title is no longer in print, I have included some poems from it as well.

I have retained Masters' use of the now-outdated Wade-Giles transliterations of Chinese words and names. Since in many cases the newer systems have updated our pronunciations as well, I thought it best to preserve the sounds and spellings originally intended by Masters, as an American poet writing in the first half of the twentieth century.

Where poems I have chosen appeared in more than one of Masters' collections, I have assigned them to the earliest book in which they are included. For example, "Lines Written in the Desplaines Forest," from Masters' first book, reappears twenty years later in *The Great Valley*, its title shortened to "The Desplaines Forest," but otherwise unchanged.

Like Herbert Russell and John Hallwas before me, I have taken the liberty of making a number of silent corrections to Masters' frequently erratic punctuational efforts and disagreements in verb tense or number. My own sense, from working intimately with these poems over many years, is that Masters' ear was quicker than either his eye or his hand. Because the voice and cadence are nearly always quite clear when a piece is read aloud, I have preferred to alter punctuation rather than word forms wherever possible. However, in some instances, the grammatical snarls have necessitated revisions to a phrase, a line, or in some cases an entire sentence. For example, here is a passage from the title poem in Masters' 1919 collection, *Starved Rock*, as it originally appeared in the Macmillan edition:

> The eagles and the Indians left it here
> In solitude, blown clean
> Of kindred things: as an oak whose leaves are sere
> Fly over the valley when the winds are keen,
> And nestle where the earth receives
> Another generation of exhausted leaves.

Since the word "oaks" is plural and therefore cannot be the subject for the verb "fly"—and since, in any case, oaks cannot fly (at least in an essentially realistic poem)—it seemed obvious that "leaves" was the intended grammatical subject. Therefore, I amended the passage as follows:

> The eagles and the Indians left it here
> In solitude, blown clean
> Of kindred things: as an oak whose leaves, all sere,
> Fly over the valley when the winds are keen....

In a few instances I have gone further, perhaps exceeding my remit. For example, about two-thirds of the way through "Ulysses" (from *The Open Sea*), there is a line which becomes a sort of refrain at the end of four consecutive stanzas (five if one counts a variation after the fourth). Here is its first iteration, as originally printed:

> "We dined in grottoes of blooming ivy;
> We supped in halls of cedar and gold.
> We slept on balconies, sapphire-tented—
> But even I found this growing old.

Metrical substitutions in the first three lines are easy for the reader to negotiate and add energy. But in that fourth line the additional unstressed syllable could legitimately belong to any foot but the first, and no choice seems right. Are we supposed to shift the stress from "I" to "found"? If not, do we shift it from "this" to the first syllable of "growing"? Since the first three lines of the stanza *are* so good metrically, the stumble is even more noticeable by contrast, and the three repetitions which follow call even more attention to it. I therefore substituted this rearrangement:

> But even this, I found, grew old.

What my version lacks in vigor I believe it makes up for in ease of comprehension. Bringing "even" and "this" together allows the stresses to work with the meaning instead of against it. Changing the verb from "growing" to "grew" also creates a closer echo of the variation that follows the four exact repetitions: "Empty promises too grow old." The reader will note that every word from the original line appears in my revision of it; only the form of the verb has been altered.

In the interests of full disclosure, I should also mention that there were a few passages in the longer poems where the original grammar or phrasing were so garbled that no sense could be made of them. This, I suspect, was largely due to Masters' tendency toward extraordinarily long, additive sentence constructions in these discursive poems: he simply lost his way grammatically. In these instances I made small cuts, none of which exceeds four lines or disturbs the form, the meter, or the sense of the piece in question.

Masters' biographer Herbert Russell notes that the poet "usually depended on his editors to look after such things" (*ELM* 9). If so, it seems obvious that he was poorly served by them. As I hope will be clear, the sole purpose of my own interventions has been to catch what no responsible editor should have missed in the first place. Since this book is intended for general readers rather than scholars, I hope that my intrusions on the texts may be forgiven.

Ryan Guth<br>
Jackson State Community College<br>
July 15, 2021

# Works Cited

Flanagan, John T. *Edgar Lee Masters: The Spoon River Poet and His Critics.* Scarecrow Press, 1974.

Hallwas, John E. "Introduction." *Spoon River Anthology: An Annotated Edition.* University of Illinois Press, 1992, pp. 1-79.

Masters, Edgar Lee. *Across Spoon River.* With an introduction by Ronald Primeau. University of Illinois Press, 1991.

---. *The Living Thoughts of Emerson.* Selected and with an introduction by Masters. Longmans, 1940.

---. *Whitman.* Scribner's, 1937.

Primeau, Ronald. *Beyond Spoon River: The Legacy of Edgar Lee Masters.* University of Texas Press, 1981.

Russell, Herbert K. "After *Spoon River*: Masters' Poetic Development 1916-1919." *The Vision of This Land: Studies of Vachel Lindsay, Edgar Lee Masters, and Carl Sandburg.* Ed. John E. Hallwas and Dennis J. Reader. Western Illinois University Press, 1976.

---. *Edgar Lee Masters: A Biography.* University of Illinois Press, 2001.

from
*A Book of Verses*

(1898)

## LINES WRITTEN IN THE DESPLAINES FOREST

The sun has sunk below the level plain,
And yet above the forest's leafy gloom
The glory of the evening lightens still.
Smooth as a mirror is the river's face
With Heaven's light, and all its radiant clouds
And shadows which against the river's shore
Already are as night. From retreat
Obscure and lonely, evening's saddest bird
Whistles, and beyond the water comes
The musical reply, and silence reigns—
Save for the noisy chorus of the frogs,
And undistinguished sounds of faint portent
That night has come.
     There is a rustic bridge
That spans the stream, from which we look below
At heaven above; 'till revery reclaims
The mind from hurried thought, and merges it
Into the universal mind which broods
O'er such a scene.
     Strange quietude o'erspreads
The restless flame of being, and the soul
Beholds its source and destiny, and feels
Not sorrowful to sink into the breast
Of that large life whereof it is a part.
What are we? But the question is not solved
Here in the presence of intensest thought,
Where nature stills the clamor of the world
And leaves us in communion with ourselves.
Hence, to the strivings of the clear-eyed day,
What take we that shall mitigate the pangs
That each soul is alone, and that all friends
Gentle and wise and good can never soothe
The ache of the subconscious, which is
Something unfathomed and unmedicined?
Yet this it is which keeps us in the path
Of some ambition, cherished or pursued;
The still, small voice that is not quieted
By disregard, but ever speaks to us

Its mandates while we wake or sleep, and asks
A closer harmony with that great scheme
Which is the music of the universe.

So as the cherubim of Heaven defend
The realms of the unknown with flaming swords,
Thence are we driven to the world which is
Ours to be known through Art, who beckons us
To excellence, and in her rarer moods
Casts shadowy glances toward serener lands
Where all the serious gods, removed from stress
And interruption, build as we conceive:
In fellowship that knows not that reserve
Which clouds the hearts of those who wish to live,
As they, in that large realm of perfect mind.

## BYRON

These are the falls men name St. Anthony:
    This is the mighty Mississippi's source.
    And I have watched with what tempestuous force
These torrents plunge and struggle to be free
Among sharp rocks their vexéd destiny.
    But where the waters of the gulf are hoarse,
    Dim, vast, intent, this river takes its course
Still as the surface of a charméd sea.

There was a man of strong and passionate youth,
    Clothed with the might of waters which o'er-leapt
    The bounds of time; and had he only kept
That stream of life which deepens toward the mouth
    Of the eternal seas, then had they swept
Flecked with a thousand stars of patient truth!

# BALLADE OF SALEM TOWN

Where is the Inn of Salem Town,
    Where Lincoln loafed ere we knew his name;
When the Clarys from Prairie Grove were down,
    And he kindled mirth with his wit like flame?
    Loud are these things on the lips of fame,
But crumbled to dust is the log-wood wall,
    And perished alike are 'squire and dame—
The toiling year is the Lord of all.

Where is the mill of such renown?
    And the sluice where swirling waters came?
And the hamlet's sage, and the rustic clown,
    And those who had glory, and those who had shame?
    And those who lost in this curious game:
The bully, the acred-lord, and his thrall?
    Gone are they all, beyond Time's reclaim—
The toiling year is the Lord of all.

But when jest passed 'twist laggard and lown,
    And the cold wind whined at the window frame;
Then careless alike of smile or frown,
    He builded for those who should carp or blame.
    Thereafter, when Error should seek to maim
The hand of Liberty in her hall,
    When he made Malice and Treason tame—
The toiling year is the Lord of all.

    ENVOY
Prince! this shaft of marble is brown
    Ere a cycle is past, and at last will fall;
But fame has fashioned his fadeless crown:
    The toiling year is the Lord of all.

from
*The Blood of the Prophets*

(1905)

self-published under the pseudonym "Dexter Wallace"

## BALLAD OF THE TRAITOR'S SOUL

'Twas the shrunken soul of the traitor
    That whined in a coign of the dark,
And the fiends were aroused from slumber
    When Cerberus began to bark.

"Methought that I spoke," said Julian,
    Who betrayed God's own demesne;
"And I," said the ghost of Caesar,
    "Heard the dying groans of the slain."

"'Twas the voice," said the high priest Caiaphas,
    "That uttered those words of awe:
'Ye have given a tithe of anise,
    And broken the weightier law.'"

Then cried out Judas Iscariot,
    Who fled on the wings of the wind,
"Someone is counting the silver
    And wailing because I sinned."

But spake up the seven devils,
    That vexed Mary Magdalene:
"The days of our bondage are over;
    We are no longer unclean!"

"Moreover, the voice that called us
    Said, 'Enter the souls of men,
For Belial rules this cycle,
    And Mammon has triumphed again.'"

Then the horrent jowls of Moloch
    Wrinkled into a grin,
And he growled, "'Tis the soul of the traitor;
    Open and let him in."

'Twas the shrunken soul of the traitor,
    Like a mouse at the furnace door,
That stood in the haze of Hades
    And trembled within its roar.

Then rose up the form of Satan
    Who, taking a crucible, saith
"The shrunken soul of the traitor
    Shall suffer the second death."

"Come, anarchs of ancient cities,
    And captains of torch and sword,
For hell hath never received one
    By God and by fiends so abhorred!"

Then the shrunken soul of the traitor
    Pleaded that he might live:
"Ye have borne with Phillip and Herod,
    So my sin ye ought to forgive."

But Phillip came forward and mocked him:
    *"The laws of God may atone*
*The crime of destroying a country,*
    *Unless he destroys his own."*

Then the horrent jowls of Moloch
    Wrinkled into a grin;
And, the crucible being ready,
    They threw the renegade in—

And fed the fire beneath him,
    Until in the crucible lay
A drop of green, bitter water
    That smelled of death and decay.

Then Satan seized hold of the crucible
    And drained that drop on the fire,
And a flame leaped up to the heavens
    And instantly did expire.

And there in the darkness that followed,
    The arch-fiends with broken breath
Fled from that place of horror
    And the sight of the second death.

## EPITAPH FOR A DEAD SENATOR

Alas! he died when swill flowed far and near,
    While there were other pearls and deeper mud.
Muse of the belly, drop a briny tear—
    The educated hog has crossed the flood.

from
*Songs and Sonnets*

(1910)

self-published under the pseudonym "Webster Ford"

## LOVE'S PHILOSOPHY

Straight rows of stricken summer grass,
Wan Heloise, about you stand
Where the sunbeams, sick and drifting, pass
In this remote and silent land.

From solemn fields and soundless woods,
From hollows of the dreaming hills,
The spirits of these solitudes—
The souls of vanished daffodils—

Hover about you, Heloise,
Because your mood to them is meet
Who see in your deep eyes the lees
Of emptied summer's ruddy heat.

Pale Heloise, against your gown
Of ashen pearl, the purple phlox
Brush as you walk the garden down,
Filled with the withered hollyhocks:

Your garden now a pensive ghost
Beneath the unchanging skies which make
The heart long for a summer lost,
And make wild fancies ache and ache.

For what? Ah, Heloise, for what?
For the vague bliss that is not ours,
And leaves us stung that it is not;
For life's great love that mocks our powers;

For yourself who in these trembling days
Seek for a joy that flamed from earth—
And barren left your after-ways,
Who missed your heart's desire and mirth.

Choking within your ripened breast,
Life's passionate voice would speak in rhyme
From which, were it silenced, you would rest
As the earth rests in autumn time.

No more of mystic grief. Behold,
For us the blood-red tide is high!
For us the wine, for us the gold,
For us awhile the summer sky!

Leave your sad garden to the past;
Put on your gown of gold and red—
Feast, ere shall come the days of fast;
Live, ere the time of life be sped!

Some hidden bower contains for us
A scroll of verses and a lute,
Where the warm winds melodious
Drop to our hands the finished fruit.

Where we two in a sudden spell
May bring down heaven with a kiss,
And know all things desirable
In one great moment's perfect bliss.

Bright Heloise, you raise your head:
Your lips are dumb, your heart leaps up—
You leave the meadows of the dead—
Life tenders, and you take, the cup!

# ETERNAL WOMAN

Within her face I read myself
Remembered, passed from thought:
She is the hope that spurred my youth;
She is the grace I sought.
Her tears reveal the good I missed
And blot the ill I wrought.

Amidst these later years I stood
Where souls laugh down their care.
Here it was strange again to see
Love's vernal face and fair;
She is the Life that brought to life
Youth's wild and sweet despair.

A languid bliss, a vanished dream,
Her eyes make new and sweet.
She soothes with words a thwarted heart
Lettered in time's defeat.
She is the hyaline cup that makes
The quiet pulses beat.

Between us pass the arisen years,
And wounded joys restore.
All shy delights, all wingéd moods,
Open for her the door.
She is the Nereid voice that woke
Music's forgotten lore.

She is the mystery of the world
Strayed out from heaven above;
The light that lures beyond the sky
The souls foredoomed to rove.
And if she slay us it is well,
For she is Life and Love.

from
*Songs and Sonnets, 2nd Series*

(1912)

self-published under the pseudonym "Webster Ford"

## PAST AND PRESENT

Past midnight! Vastly overhead
A wash of stars—the town's asleep,
And through the pine trees of the dead
The mystic winds of morning creep.

Dim 'mid the hillside's shadowed grass,
I count the marble slabs. How vain
My throbbing life that waits to pass
Into the great world on the train!

The city's vision fades from mind.
I only see the hill and sky,
And on the mist that rides the wind
A tottering pageant meets my eye.

The cock crows faintly, far away;
A troop of age and grief appears.
Ye shadows of a distant day,
What do ye, pioneers?

There shines the engine's comet light.
Ye shadows of a century, set,
Haste to the hillside and the night—
I am not of you yet!

# THE WORLD SPIRIT

I am the world spirit speaking:
Let the nations take heed.
The slow, dumb ages are wreaking
The strength of my creed.
Armies and strength of battle
And the glory of peace—
They are the slaughter of cattle
That give me increase.

Ye have seen from the ages olden,
Though the beast of war
Suffers himself to be holden,
And Christ is the Czar,
That I, like the morning breezes,
Move with the sun.
The world does naught that it pleases;
I will what is done!

Dismantle your ships of thunder;
I will clothe them again.
Strengthen your armies for plunder;
I will destroy your men.
Hate and love and glory,
Hands that caress and smite—
What is not transitory?
The world and my might!

And this I say; I have sworn it:
What has been shall never more be.
The golden age? You may mourn it,
But who would stay the tide of the sea?
The world, through folly and sorrow,
Must move with the morning star;
And Progress, through every tomorrow,
Is my Avatar.

from
*Songs and Satires*

(1916)

# SILENCE

    I have known the silence of the stars and of the sea,
And the silence of the city when it pauses,
And the silence of a man and a maid,
And the silence for which music alone finds the word,
And the silence of the woods before the winds of the spring begin,
And the silence of the sick
When their eyes roam about the room.
And I ask: For the depths,
Of what use is language?
A beast of the field moans a few times
When death takes its young,
And we are voiceless in the presence of realities—
We cannot speak.

    A curious boy asks an old soldier,
Sitting in front of the grocery store,
"How did you lose your leg?"
And the old soldier is struck with silence,
Or his mind flies away,
Because he cannot concentrate it on Gettysburg.
It comes back jocosely
And he says, "A bear bit it off."
And the boy wonders, while the old soldier
Dumbly, feebly, lives over
The flashes of guns, the thunder of cannon,
The shrieks of the slain,
And himself lying on the ground;
And the hospital surgeons, the knives,
And the long days in bed.
But if he could describe it all,
He would be an artist.
But if he were an artist, there would be deeper wounds
Which he could not describe.

There is the silence of a great hatred,
And the silence of a great love,
And the silence of a deep peace of mind,
And the silence of an embittered friendship.
There is the silence of a spiritual crisis
Through which your soul, exquisitely tortured,
Comes with visions not to be uttered
Into a realm of higher life.
And the silence of the gods who understand each other without
    speech.
There is the silence of defeat.
There is the silence of those unjustly punished,
And the silence of the dying whose hand
Suddenly grips yours.
There is the silence between father and son,
When the father cannot explain his life
Even though he be misunderstood for it.

    There is the silence that comes between husband and wife.
There is the silence of those who have failed,
And the vast silence that covers
Broken nations and vanquished leaders.
There is the silence of Lincoln,
Thinking of the poverty of his youth.
And the silence of Napoleon
After Waterloo.
And the silence of Jeanne d'Arc
Saying amid the flames, "Blessed Jesus"—
Revealing in two words all sorrow, all hope.
And there is the silence of age,
Too full of wisdom for the tongue to utter it
In words intelligible to those who have not lived
The great range of life.

    And there is the silence of the dead.
If we who are in life cannot speak
Of profound experiences,
Why do you marvel that the dead
Do not tell you of death?
Their silence shall be interpreted
As we approach them.

# THE SIGN

There's not a soul on the square,
And the snow blows up like a sail
Or dizzily drifts like a drunken man,
Falling before the gale.

And when the wind eddies it rifts
The snow that lies in drifts;
And it skims along the walk and sifts
In stairways, doorways, all about
The steps of the church in an angry rout.
And one would think that a hungry hound
Was out in the cold, for the sound.

But I do not seem to mind
The snow that makes one blind,
Nor the crying voice of the wind.
I hate to hear the creak of the sign
Of Harmon Whitney, attorney at law,
With its rhythmic monotone of awe,
And neither a moan nor yet a whine,
Nor a cry of pain—one can't define
The sound of a creaking sign,

Especially if the sky be bleak
And no one stirs, however you seek.
Yet every time you hear it creak,
You wonder why they leave it stay
When the man is buried and hidden away
Many a day!

## IN THE CAGE

The sounds of midnight trickle into the roar
Of morning, over the water growing blue.
At ten o'clock the August sunbeams pour
A blinding flood on Michigan Avenue.

But yet the half-drawn shades of bottle green
Leave the recesses of the room
With misty auras drawn around their gloom,
Where things lie undistinguished, scarcely seen.

You, standing between the window and the bed,
Are edged with rainbow colors. And I lie
Drowsy, with quizzical half-open eye
Musing upon the contour of your head,
Watching you comb your hair:
Clothed in a corset waist, and skirt of silk
Which reaches to your knees and makes your bare
And delicate legs, by contrast, white as milk.
And as you toss your head to comb its tresses,
They flash upon me like long stripes of sand
Between a moonlit sea, pale as your hand,
And a red sun that on a high dune stresses
Its sanguine heat.         And then at times your lips—
Protruding, half unconscious, half in scorn—
Engage my eyes while looking through the morn
At the clear oval of your brow, brought full
Over the sovereign largeness of your eyes;
Or at your breasts that shake not as you pull
The comb through stubborn tangles, only rise,
Scarcely perceptible, with breath or sighs:
Firm, unmaternal, like a young Bacchante's;
Or at your nose, profoundly dipped like Dante's
Over your chin that softly melts away.

Now you seem fully under my heart's sway;
I have slipped through the magic of your mesh,
Freed once again and strengthened by your flesh.
You seem a weak thing for a strong man's play.
Yet I know now that we shall scarce have parted
When I shall think of you, half heavy-hearted.
I know our partings. You will faintly smile
And look at me with eyes that have no guile,
Or have too much, and pass into the sphere
Where you keep independent life meanwhile.
How do you live without me, is the fear?
You do not lean upon me, ask my love, or wonder
Of other loves I may have hidden under
These casual renewals of our love.
And if I loved you, I should lie in flame
And go about re-murmuring your name;
And these are things a man should be above.

Yet as I lie here on the imminent brink
Of soul's surrender into your soul's power,
And in the white light of the morning hour,
I see what life would be if we should link
Our lives together in a marriage pact:
For we would walk along a boundless tract
Of perfect hell; but your disloyalty
Would be of spirit, for I have not won,
Mastered and bound, your spirit unto me.
And if you had a lover in the way
I have you, it would not by half betray
My love as does your vague and chainless thought
Which wanders, soars or vanishes, returns,
Changes, astonishes; or chills, or burns,
Is unresisting, plastic, freely wrought
Under my hands; yet to no unison
Of my life and of yours.
                    Upon this brink
I watch you now, and think
Of all that has been preached or sung or spoken
Of woman's tragedy in woman's fall;
And all the pictures of a woman broken
By man's superior strength.

          Yet there you stand,
Your heart and life as firmly in command
Of your resolve as mine is, knowing all
Of man the master, and his power to harm,
His rulership of spheres material,
Bread, customs, rules of fair repute—
What are they all against your slender arm
Which long since plucked the fruit
Of good and evil, and of life at last,
And now of Life? For, dancing, you have cast
Veil after veil of ideals or pretense
With which men clothe the being feminine
To satisfy their lordship, or their sense
Of ownership, and hide the things of sin.
You have thrown them aside, veil after veil,
And there you stand: unarmored, weirdly frail,
Yet strong as nature, making comical
The poems and the tales of woman's fall . . . .

You nod your head, you smile; I feel the air
Made by the closing door. I lie and stare
At it, now shut. One—two—your tufted steps
Die on the velvet of the outer hall.
You have escaped. And I would not pursue,
Though we are but caged creatures, I and you:
A male and female tiger in a zoo.
For I shall wait you. Life himself will track
Your wanderings and bring you back,
And shut you up again with me, and cage
Our love and hatred, and our silent rage.

from
*The Great Valley*

(1916)

TO THE MEMORY

OF

SQUIRE DAVIS AND LUCINDA MASTERS

WHO, CLOSE TO NATURE, ONE IN DEEP RELIGIOUS FAITH, THE OTHER
IN PANTHEISTIC RAPTURE AND HEROISM, LIVED NEARLY A
HUNDRED YEARS IN THIS LAND OF ILLINOIS,
I INSCRIBE

THE GREAT VALLEY

IN ADMIRATION OF THEIR GREAT STRENGTH, MASTERY
OF LIFE, HOPEFULNESS, CLEAR AND
BEAUTIFUL DEMOCRACY

EDGAR LEE MASTERS

# THE MOURNER'S BENCH

They're holding a revival at New Hope Meeting house.
I can't keep from going; I ought to stay away.
For I come home and toss in bed till day
For thinking of my sin, and the trouble I am in.
I dream I hear the dancers
In the steps and swings,
The quadrilles and the lancers
They danced at Revis Springs.
I lie and think of Charley, Charley, Charley,
The Bobtown dandy
Who had his way with me.
And no one is so handy
A dancer as Charley
To "Little Drops of Brandy,"
Or "The Wind that Shakes the Barley,"
Or "Good mornin' Uncle Johnny, I've Fetched your Wagon Home."

And Greenberry Atterberry, who toed it like a pigeon,
Has gone and got religion;
He's deserted the dancers, the fiddlers, the merry-makers,
And I should do it too.
For Charley, Charley has left me for to roam.
But a woman at the mourner's bench must tell her story true—
What shall I do? What shall I do?

My grandmother told me of Old Peter Cartwright,
Who preached hell-fire
And the worm that never dies.
And here's a young preacher at the New Hope Meeting house,
And every one allows he has old Peter's brows,
And the flaming of the eyes,
And the very same way, they say.
Last night he stuck his finger right down in my direction
And said: "God doesn't care
For your woman's hair.
Jesus wants to know if your soul is fair
As your woman's complexion."
And then I thought he knew—

O, what shall I do?

Greenberry Atterberry, weeping and unsteady,
Had left his seat already.
He stood at the mourner's bench in great tribulation
And told the congregation
That fiddling and dancing and tobacco chewin'
Led up to whiskey and to woman's ruin—
And I thought he looked at me.
Well, you can stop dancing, and you can stop drinking,
And you can leave the quarter-horses at the crooked races.
But a woman, a woman—the people will be thinking
Forever of a woman who confesses her behavior.
And then I couldn't look in the people's faces,
All weeping and singing "O Gentle Savior!"
Then the devil said: "You wench,
You'd cut a pretty figure at the mourner's bench.
Go out and look for Charley,
Go out and look for Charley,
He's down at Leese's Grove.
He has found a fresh love—
Go win him back again.
He is dancing on the platform to 'The Speckled Hen.'"

O Savior, Savior, how can I join the mourners,
Face all the scorners?
How can I hunt for Charley at Leese's Grove?
How can I stand the staring, the whispering of things
Down at Revis Springs?
How can I stand the mocking of the fiddle strings?
Charley! Charley!
So it's knowing what's best to do,
Savior! Savior!
It's knowing what's best to do!

# THE GOSPEL OF MARK

How long have you been waiting? Not so long?
I'm glad of that. You found the place at once.
Well, there's the Campus Martius. When you're there
You see, above this, Collus Hortulorum;
A good place for two men like us to meet.
Here's where luxurious souls have their abodes.
That's Sallust's garden there. They do not care
So much about us as some others do.
There is a tolerance comes from being rich;
An urbane soul is fashioned by a villa.
Our faith is not to these a wicked thing,
A deadly superstition as some deem it.
But Mark, my son, there's Rome below you there —
What temples, arches, under the full moon!
Here let us sit, beside this chestnut tree,
And while the soft wind blows out of the sea
Let's finish up our talks. You must know all
Wherewith to write the story, ere I die
Beneath the wrath of Nero. See that light,
Faint like a little candle—I passed there.
That's one of our poor men: they make us lamps,
Wherewith to light the streets and Nero's gardens!
Yet we shall be lamps they'll wish to snuff in time.

We met to-night at one Silvanus' house.
And I was telling them about the night
When in Gethsemane you followed Him,
Having a cloth around your naked body,
And how you laid hold on Him, left the cloth
And fled. But when you write this, you can say
"A certain young man," leaving out your name.
You might not wish to have it known 'twas you
Who ran away, as I would like to hide
How I fell into sleep and failed to watch,
And afterwards declared I knew Him not.
But as for me, omit no thing. The world
Will gain for seeing me rise out of weakness
To strength, and out of fear to boldness. Time

Has wrought his wonders in me: I am rock!
Let hell beat on me, I shall stand from now!

And don't forget the first man that He healed.
There's deep significance in this, my son,
That first of all He'd take an unclean spirit
And cast it out. Then second was my mother:
Cured of her fever, just as you might say.
Be rid of madness, things that tear and plague,
Then cool you of the fever of vain life.
But don't forget to write how He would say
"Tell no man of this." Say that and no more—
Though I may think He said it lest the crowds
That followed Him would take his strength for healing,
And leave no strength for words, let be and write
"Tell no man of this," simply. For you see,
These madmen quieted, these lepers cleansed,
Had soon to die; all now are dead, perhaps.
And with them ends their good. But what He said
Remains for generations yet to come, with power
To heal and heal. My son, preserve your notes
Of what I've told you, even above your life.
Make many copies, lest one script be lost.
I shall not to another tell it all
As I have told it you.
                    But as for me,
What merit have I that I saw and said
"Thou art the Christ?" One sees the thing he sees.
That is a matter of the eye—behold,
What is the eye? Is there an Eye Power which
Produces eyes, a primal source of seeing,
An ocean of beholding? As the ocean
Makes rivers, streams and pools, so does this Power
Make eyes? You take an egg and keep it warm
About a day, then break the shell and look:
You'll find dark spots on either side of what will be eyes
In season, but just now they cannot see,
Although the Eye Power back of them can see
Both what they are and how to make them eyes
By giving them its quality and strength.
And all the time, while these dark spots emerge

From yolk to eyes, this Rome is here no less,
This moon, these stars, this wonder! Take a child:
It stares at flowers and tears them, or again
It claws the whiteness of its mother's breast,
Sees nothing but the things beneath its nose.
The world around it lies here to be seen,
And will be seen from boyhood on to age
In different guises, aspects, richnesses,
According to the man. For every man
Sees different from his fellow. What's an eye?
I say not "what's an eye," but what is here
For eyes to see? What wonders in that sky
Beyond my eye! What living things concealed
Beneath my feet in grass or moss or slime,
As small to crickets as they are to us!
For Nero at the Circus holds a ruby
Before his eye, to give his eye more sight
To see the games and tortures. Thus I say
There was no merit in me when I said
"Thou art the Christ."
                    Let's think of eyes this way:
The lawyers said there's nothing in this fellow.
His family behold no wonder in Him.
Have Mary Magdalene and I invented
These words, this story?—and who are we to do so,
A fallen woman and a fisherman?
Or did it happen? Did we see these things?
Did Mary see Him risen, and did I?
Were other eyes still dark spots on the yolk,
And were our eyes full grown? and did we see?
Is this a madman's world where I can talk,
And have you write for centuries to read,
And play the fool with them? Or do all things
Of spirit, as of stars, of spring and growth,
Proceed in order, under law, to ends?
No, Mark, my son, this is the truth—so write,
Preserve this story taken from my lips.
My work is almost done. Rome is the end
Of all my labors; I have faith The Eye
Will give me other eyes for other worlds!

Why should I not believe this? Not all seasons
Are for unfolding. In the winter time
You cannot see the miracle of birth,
Of germinating seeds, of blossoming.
Why not, then, that one time for seeing Death
Go up like mist before the rising sun?
And in this single instance of our Lord
Arising from the grave, see all men rise,
And all men's souls discovered in his soul:
Their quality and essence, their strength, made clear?
And why not I the seer of these things?
Why should there be another and not I?
And I declare to you that untold millions,
In centuries untold, will live and die
By these words which you write as I have said them.
And nation after nation will be moulded,
As heated wax is moulded, by these words.
And spirits in their inmost power will feel
Change and regeneration through them!
                                                Well, what then?
Do you say God is living, that this world,
These constellations, move by law, that all
This miracle of life and light is held
In harmony, and that the soul of man
Moves *not* in order, but that it's allowed
To prove an anarch to itself? sole thing
That turns upon itself, sole thing that's shown
The path that leads no-whither? is allowed
To feed on falsehood? is allowed, even,
To wander lawless to its ruin, fooled
By what it craves, by what it feels, by eyes
That swear the truth of what they see? by words
Which you will write from words I have affirmed?
And do you say that Life shall prove the foe
Of life, and Law of law? Or do you say
That child's eyes see reality which see
The poppy blossoms, or the mother's breast;
Yet that this Rome, these stars, do not exist
Because the child's eyes cannot compass them
And get their image?
                  No, it cannot be.
Man's soul, the chiefest flower of all we know,

Is not the toy of Malice or of Sport.
It is not set apart to be betrayed,
Or gulled to its undoing, left to dash
Its hopeless head against this rock's exception;
No water for its thirst, no Life to feed it,
No law to guide it, though this universe
Is under Law; no God to mark its steps
Except the God of worlds and suns and stars
Who loves it not: loves worlds and suns and stars
And them alone, and leaves the soul to pass
Unfathered—lets me have a madman's dream,
And gives it such reality that I
Take fire and light the world, convincing eyes
Left foolish to believe. It cannot be. . . .

Go write what I have told you, come what will.
I'm going to the catacombs to pray.

from
*Toward the Gulf*

(1918)

## TOMORROW IS MY BIRTHDAY

Well then, another drink! Ben Jonson knows,
And so do you, Michael Drayton, that to-morrow
I reach my fifty-second year. But hark ye,
To-morrow lacks two days of being a month—
Here is a secret—since I made my will!
Heigh ho! That's done too! I wonder why I did it?
That I should make a will! Yet it may be
That Heaven inspired the deed.
                           As a mad younker,
I knew an aged man in Warwickshire
Who used to say "Ah, mercy me," for sadness
Of change, or passing time, or secret thoughts.
If it was spring he sighed it, if 'twas fall,
With drifting leaves, he looked upon the rain
And with that doleful suspiration kept
This habit of his grief. And on a time,
As he stood looking at the flying clouds,
I loitering near, expectant, heard him say it,
And asked, "Why do you say 'Ah, mercy me,'
Now that it's April?" But he hobbled off
And left me empty there.
                       Now here am I!
Oh, it is strange to find myself this age
And rustling like a peascod, though unshelled,
And like that aged man of Warwickshire
Slaved by a mood which must have breath—"Tra-la!"
That's what I say for his "Ah, mercy me."
For look you, Ben, I catch myself with "Tra-la"
The moment I break sleep to see the day.
At work, alone — vexed, laughing, mad, or glad—
I say "Tra-la," unknowing. Oft at table
I say "Tra-la." And 'tother day, poor Anne
Looked long at me and said, "You say, 'Tra-la'
Sometimes when you're asleep; why do you so?"
And I bethought me of that aged man
Who used to say, "Ah, mercy me," but answered:
"Perhaps I am so happy when awake
The song crops out in slumber—who can say?"

And Anne arose, began to keel the pot.
But was she answered, Ben? Who knows a woman?

To-morrow is my birthday. If I die,
Slip out of this with Bacchus for a guide,
What soul would interdict the poppied way?
Heroes may look the Monster down; a child
Can wilt a lion, who is cowed to see
Such bland unreckoning of his strength—but I,
Having so greatly lived, would sink away
Unknowing my departure. I have died
A thousand times, and with a valiant soul
Have drunk the cup. But why? In such a death
Tomorrow shines, and there's a place to lean.
But in this death that has no bottom to it,
No bank beyond, no place to step, the soul
Grows sick, and like a falling dream we shrink
From that inane which gulfs us without place
For us to stand and see it.
      Yet, dear Ben,
This thing must be. That's what we live to know
Out of long dreaming, saying that we know it
As yeasty heroes in their braggart teens
Spout learnedly of war, who never saw
A cannon aimed. You drink too much today,
Or get a scratch while turning Lucy's stile,
And like a beast you sicken, like a beast
They cart you off. What matter if your thought
Outsoared the Phoenix? Like a beast you rot!
Methinks that something wants our flesh, as we
Hunger for flesh of beasts. But still, tomorrow—
Tomorrow and tomorrow and tomorrow
Creeps in this petty pace—O, Michael Drayton,
Some end must be. But 'twixt the fear of ceasing
And weariness of going on, we lie
Upon these thorns!
      These several springs I find
No new birth in the Spring. And yet in London
I used to cry "O, would I were in Stratford!
It's April and the larks are singing now;
The flags are green along the Avon river.
O, would I were a rambler in the fields!

This poor machine is racing to its wreck;
This grist of thought is endless, this old sorrow
Sprouts, winds, and crawls in London's darkness. Come
Back to your landscape! Peradventure waits
Some woman there who will make new the earth
And crown the spring with fire."
                              So back I come.
And the springs march before me, saying "Behold,
Here are we," and "what would you, can you use us?"
What good is air if lungs are out, or springs
When the mind's blown so far away no spring,
No loveliness of earth, can call it back?
I tell you what it is: in early youth,
The life is in the loins; by thirty years
It travels through the stomach to the lungs,
And then we strut and crow. By forty years,
The fruit is swelling while the leaves are fresh.
By fifty years you're ripe and begin to rot.
At fifty-two, or fifty-five, or sixty,
The life is in the seed—what's spring to you then?
Puff! Puff! You are so winged and light you fly;
With every passing zephyr are blown off
And drifting God knows where; cry out "tra-la,"
"Ah, mercy me," as it may happen you.
Puff! Puff! away you go!
                  Another drink?
Why, you may drown the earth with ale and I
Will drain it like a sea. The more I drink,
The better I see that this is April time. . . .

Ben! There is one Voice which says to everything:
"Dream what you will, I'll make you bear your seed.
And, having borne, the sickle comes among ye
And takes your stalk." The rich and sappy greens
Of spring or June show life within the loins
And all the world is fair, for now the plant
Can drink the level cup of flame where heaven
Is poured full by the sun. But when the blossom
Flutters its colors, then it takes the cup
And waves the stalk aside. And, having drunk
The stalk to penury, then slumber comes
With dreams of spring stored in the imprisoned germ,

An old life and a new life all in one:
A thing of memory and of prophecy,
Of reminiscence, longing, hope and fear.
What has been ours is taken, what was ours
Becomes entailed on our seed in the spring,
Fees in possession and enjoyment too....

The thing is sex, Ben. It is that which lives
And dies in us, makes April and unmakes,
And leaves a man like me at fifty-two,
Finished but living, on the pinnacle
Betwixt a death and birth; the earth consumed
And heaven rolled up to eyes whose troubled glances
Would shape again to something better—but what?
Give me a woman, Ben, and I will pick
Out of this April, by this larger art
Of fifty-two, such songs as we have heard,
Both you and I, when weltering in the clouds
Of that eternity which comes in sleep,
Or in the viewless spinning of the soul
When most intense. The woman is somewhere,
And that's what tortures when I think this field
So often gleaned could blossom once again:
If I could but find her!
                        Well, as to my plays:
I have not written out what I would write.
They have a thousand buds of finer flowering,
And over "Hamlet" hangs a teasing spirit
As fine to that as sense is fine to flesh.
Good friends, my soul beats up its prisoned wings
Against the ceiling of a vaster whorl,
And would break through and enter. But, fair friends,
What strength in place of sex shall steady me?
What is the motive of this higher mount?
What process in the making of myself—
The very fire, as it were, of my growth—
Shall furnish forth these writings by the way,
As incident, expression, of the nature
Relumed for adding branches, twigs, and leaves?...

Suppose I'd make a tragedy of this,
Focus my fancied "Dante" to this theme

And leave my half-writ "Sappho," which at best
Is just another delving in the mine
That gave me "Cleopatra" and the Sonnets?
If you have genius, write my tragedy
And call it "Shakespeare, Gentleman of Stratford,"
Who lost his soul amid a thousand souls,
And had to live without it, yet live with it
As wretched as the souls whose lives he lived.
Here is a play for you: poor William Shakespeare,
This moment growing drunk, the famous author
Of certain sugared sonnets and some plays,
With this machine too much to him, which started
Some years ago, and now cries him nay and runs
Even when the house shakes, and complains: "I fall,
You shake me down, my timbers break apart.
Why, if an engine must go on like this,
The building should be stronger!"
        Or to mix,
And by the mixing, unmix metaphors.
No mortal man has blood enough for brains
And stomach too, when the brain is never done
With thinking and creating.
       For, you see,
I pluck a flower, cut off a dragon's head—
Choose twixt these figures—lo, a dozen buds,
A dozen heads, out-crop. For every fancy,
Play, sonnet, what you will, I write me out
With thinking "Now I'm done;" but a hundred others
Crowd up for voices and, like twins unborn,
Kick and turn o'er for entrance to the world.
And I, poor fecund creature, who would rest
As 'twere from an importunate husband, fly
To money-lending, farming, mulberry trees,
Enclosing Welcombe fields, or idling hours
In common talk with people like the Combes.
All this to get a heartiness, a hold
On earth again, lest Heaven's Hercules,
Finding me strayed to mid-air, kicking heels
Above the mountain tops, seize on my scruff
And bear me off or strangle.
       Good my friends,
The "Tempest" is as nothing to the voice

That calls me to performance—of what, I know not.
I've planned an epic of the Asian wash
That slopped the star of Athens and put it out;
Which should all history analyze, and present
A thousand notables in the guise of life,
And show the ancient world and worlds to come
To the last blade of thought and tiniest seed
Of growth to be. With visions such as these
My spirit turns in restless ecstasy,
And this enslavéd brain is master sponge
And sucks the blood of body, hands, and feet
While my poor spirit, like a butterfly
Gummed in its shell, beats its bedraggled wings
And cannot rise.         I'm cold. God bless the ale!
God did do well to give us anodynes. . . .
So now you know why I am much alone,
And cannot fellow with Augustine Phillips,
John Heminge, Richard Burbage, Henry Condell,
And do not have them here, dear ancient friends;
Who grieve, no doubt, and wonder for changed love.
Love's not love which alters when it finds
A change of heart. But mine has changed not, only
I cannot be my old self. I blaspheme:
I hunger for broiled fish, but fly the touch
Of hands of flesh.         I am most passionate,
And long am used perplexities of love
To bemoan and to bewail. And do you wonder,
Seeing what I am, what my fate has been?
Well, hark you; Anne is sixty now, and I,
A crater which erupts, look where she stands
In lava wrinkles—eight years older than I am,
As years go, but I am a youth afire
While she is lean and slippered. It's a Fury
Which takes me sometimes, makes my hands clutch out
For virgins in their teens. O sullen fancy!
I want them not; I want the love that springs
Like flame which blots the sun, where fuel of body
Is piled in reckless generosity. . . .

You are most learn'd, Ben—Greek and Latin know,

And think me nature's child, scarce understanding
How much of physic, law, and ancient annals
I have stored up by means of studious zeal.
But pass this by, and for the braggart breath
Ensuing now, say "Will was in his cups,
Pot-valiant, boozed, corned, squiffy, obfuscated,
Crapulous, *inter pocula*, or some such.
Good sir, or so, or friend; or gentleman,
According to the phrase, or the addition
Of man and country: on my honor, Shakespeare
At Stratford, on the twenty-second of April,
Year sixteen-sixteen of our Lord, was merry—
*Videlicet*, was drunk."
     Well, where was I?—
Oh yes, at "braggart breath." And now to say it.
I believe, and speak as I would lightly speak
Of the most common thing to sense: this mind,
Which has been used by Something as I use
A quill for writing, never in this world—
In the most high and palmy days of Greece,
Or in this roaring age—has known its peer.
No soul as mine has lived, felt, suffered, dreamed,
Broke open spirit secrets, followed trails
Of passions curious, countless lives explored,
As I have done. And what are Greek and Latin,
The lore of Aristotle or Plato, to this?
Since I know them by what I am, the essence
From which their utterance came, myself a flower
Of every graft; and being in myself
The recapitulation and the complex
Of all the great. Were not brains before books?
And even geometrics in some brain
Before old Gutenberg? O fie, Ben Jonson,
If I am nature's child, am I not all?
Howe'er it be, ascribe this to the ale
And say that reason in me was a fume.
But if you honor me, as you have said,
As much as any this side idolatry,
Think, Ben, of this: That I, whate'er I be
In your regard, have come to fifty-two
Defeated in my love, who knew too well
That poets through the love of women turn

To satyrs or to gods, even as women
By the first touch of passion bloom or rot
As angels or as bawds.
                         Bethink you also
How I have felt, seen, known the mystic process
Working in man's soul from the woman soul
As part thereof in essence, spirit and flesh,
Even as a malady may be; while this thing
Is health and growth and, growing, draws all life,
All goodness, all wisdom, for its nutriment.
Till it become a vision paradisic
And a ladder of fire for climbing, its topmost
Rung a place for stepping into heaven.. . .

This I have known, but had not. Nor have I
Stood coolly off and seen the woman, used
Her blood upon my palette. No, but heaven
Commanded my strength's use to abort and slay
What grew within me, while I saw the blood
Of love untimely ripped, as 'twere a child
Killed i' the womb, a harpy or an angel
With my own blood stained.
                          As a virgin, shamed
By the swelling life unlicensed, needles it
But empties not her womb of some last shred
Of flesh which fouls the alleys of her body
And fills her wholesome nerves with poisoned sleep
And weakness to the last of life, so I
For some shame not unlike, some need of life
To rid me of this life I had conceived,
Did up and choke it too, and thence begot
A fever and a fixed debility
For killing what begot.
                       Now you see that I
Have not grown from a central dream, but grown
Despite a wound, and over the wound, and used
My flesh to heal my flesh. My love's a fever
Which longed for that which nursed the malady,
And fed on that which still preserved the ill,
The uncertain sickly appetite to please.
My reason, the physician to my love,
Angry that his prescriptions are not kept,

Has left me. And as reason is past care
I am past cure; with ever more unrest
Made frantic-mad, my thoughts as madmen's are,
And my discourse at random from the truth,
Not knowing what she is, who swore her fair
And thought her bright, who is as black as hell
And dark as night.
     But list, good gentlemen,
This love I speak of is not as a cloak
Which one may put away to wear a coat,
And doff that for a jacket, like the loves
We men are wont to have as loves or wives.
She is the very one, the soul of souls,
And when you put her on you put on light,
Or wear the robe of Nessus, poisonous fire,
Which if you tear away you tear your life,
And if you wear you fall to ashes. So
'Tis not *her* bed-vow broke, but broke my own
Which ruins me; 'tis honest faith quite lost,
And broken hope that we could find each other,
And which mean more to me and less to her.
'Tis that she could take all of me and leave me
Without a sense of loss, without a tear,
And make me fool and perjured for the oath
That swore her fair and true. I feel myself
As like a virgin who her body gives
For love of one whose love she dreams is hers,
Then wakes to find herself a toy of blood,
A dupe of prodigal breath, abandoned quite
For other conquests. For I gave myself,
And shrink for thought thereof, and for the loss
Of myself never to myself restored.
The urtication of this shame made plays
And sonnets— as you'll find, behind all deeds
That mount to greatness, anger, hate, disgust;
But, better, love.
     To hell with punks and wenches,
Drabs, mopsies, doxies, minxes, trulls and queans,
Rips, harridans and strumpets, pieces, jades.
And likewise to the eternal bonfire lechers,
Rakehells, satyrs, goats and placket-fumblers,
Gibs, breakers-in-at-catch-doors, thunder tubes.

I think I have a fever—hell and furies!
Or else this ale grows hotter i' the mouth.
Ben, if I die before you, let me waste
Richly and freely in the good brown earth,
Untrumpeted and by no bust marked out.
What good, Ben Jonson, if the world could see
What face was mine, who wrote these plays and sonnets?
Life, you have hurt me. Since Death has a veil,
I'll take that veil and hide and, like great Caesar
Who drew his bloody toga round him, depart.

Good friends, let's to the fields—I have a fever.
After a little walk, and by your pardon,
I think I'll sleep. There is no sweeter thing,
Nor fate more blessed than to sleep. Here, world,
I pass you like an orange to a child:
I can no more with you. Do what you will.
What should my care be when I have no power
To save, guide, mould you? Naughty world, you need me
As little as I need you: go your way!
Tyrants shall rise and slaughter fill the earth,
But I shall sleep. In wars and wars and wars
The ever-replenished youth of earth shall shriek
And clap their gushing wounds—but I shall sleep,
Nor earthy thunder wake me when the cannon
Shall shake the throne of Tartarus. Orators
Shall fulmine over London or America
Of rights eternal, parchments, sacred charters;
And cut each other's throats when reason fails—
But I shall sleep. This globe may last and breed
The race of men till Time cries out "How long?"
But I shall sleep ten thousand thousand years.
I am a dream, Ben, out of a blessed sleep—
Let's walk and hear the lark.

  \*  \*  \*  \*  \*

from
*Starved Rock*

(1919)

## STARVED ROCK

As a soul from whom companionships subside,
The meaningless onsweeping tide
Of the river—hastening, as it would disown
Old ways and places—left this stone
Of sand above the valley, to look down
Miles of the valley, hamlet, village, town.

\*     \*     \*     \*     \*

It is the head-gear of a chief whose head,
Down from the implacable brow,
Waiting is held below
The waters, feather-decked
With blossoms blue and red,
With ferns and vines:
Hiding beneath the waters, head erect,
His savage eyes and treacherous designs.

\*     \*     \*     \*     \*

It is a musing memory and memorial
Of geologic ages
Before the floods began to fall;
The cenotaph of sorrows, pilgrimages
Of Marquette and LaSalle.
The eagles and the Indians left it here
In solitude, blown clean
Of kindred things: as an oak whose leaves, all sere,
Fly over the valley when the winds are keen
And nestle where the earth receives
Another generation of exhausted leaves.

\*     \*     \*     \*     \*

Fatigued with age, its sleepless eyes look over
Fenced fields of corn and wheat,
Barley and clover.
The lowered pulses of the river beat
Invisibly by the shores that stray
In progress and retreat
Past Utica and Ottawa,

And past the meadow where the Illini
Shouted and danced under the autumn moon;
When toddlers and babes gave cry,
And dogs were barking for the boon
Of the hunter, home again to clamorous tents
Smoking beneath the evening's copper sky.
Later, a remnant of the Illini
Climbed up this Rock to die
Of hunger or thirst; or down its sheer ascents
Rushed on the spears of Pottawatomies
And found the peace
Where thirst and hunger are unknown.

  *  *  *  *  *

This is the tragic and the fateful stone,
*Le Rocher* or Starved Rock:
A symbol and a paradigm,
A sphinx of elegy and battle hymn
Whose lips unlock
Life's secret, which is vanishment, defeat,
In epic dirges for the races
That pass and leave no traces
Before new generations, driven in the blast
Of Time and Nature blowing round its head—
Renewing in the Present what the Past
Knew wholly, or in part, so to repeat
Warfare, extermination, old things dead
But brought to life again
In Life's immortal pain.

  *  *  *  *  *

What destinies confer
And, laughing, mock
LaSalle, his dreamings stir
To wander here, depart
The fortress of *Creve Coeur*,
Of "broken heart,"
For this fort of Starved Rock?
After the heart is broken, then the cliff
Where vultures flock,
And where below its steeps the savage in his skiff
Cuts with pitiless knife the rope let down

For water. From the earth this Indian town
Vanished; on this Rock the Illini,
Thirsting, their buckets taken with the knife,
Lay down to die.

  \*  \*  \*  \*  \*

This is the land where every generation
Lets down its buckets for the water of Life.
We are the children and the epigone
Of the Illini, the vanished nation.
And this starved scarp of stone
Is now the emblem of our tribulation,
The inverted cup of our insatiable thirst:
The Illini, by fate accursed,
Lost this land to the Pottawatomies,
Who lost the land to us—
Who now, baffled and idolatrous
And thirsting, spurred by hope,
Kneel upon aching knees
And with our eager hands draw up the bucketless rope.

  \*  \*  \*  \*  \*

This is the tragic, the symbolic, face,
*Le Rocher* or Starved Rock,
Round which the eternal turtles drink and swim,
And serpents green and strange;
As race comes after race,
War after war.
This is the sphinx whose Memnon lips breathe dirges
Over empire's wayward star,
And the race's restless urges
Whose lips unlock
Life's secret, which is vanishment and change.

# WILD BIRDS

The wild birds among the reeds
Cry, exult, and stretch their wings.
Out of the sky they drift
And sink to the water's rushes.
But the wild birds beat their wings and cry
To the newcomer out of the sky!

Is he a stranger, this wild bird out of the sky?
Or do they cry to him because of remembered places,
And remembered days
Spent together
In the north-land, or the south-land?

Is this the ecstasy of renewal,
Or the ecstasy of beginning?
For the wild bird touches his bill
Against a mate;
He brushes her wing with his wing;
He quivers with delight
For the cool sky of blue
And the touch of her wing!

The wild birds fly up from the reeds,
Some for the south,
Some for the north.
They are gone—
Lost in the sky!

In what water do these mates of a morning
Exult on the morrow?
What wild birds will cry to them as they sink
Out of an unknown sky?
To whose cry will she quiver
Through her burnished wings to-morrow,
In the north-land,
In the south-land,
Far away?

## OH YOU SABBATARIANS!

Oh you sabbatarians, methodists, and puritans;
You bigots, devotees, and ranters;
You formalists, pietists and fanatics,
Teetotalers and hydropots;
You thin ascetics, androgynous souls,
Chaste and epicene spirits—
Eyes blind to color, ears deaf to sound,
Fingers insensitive—
Do what you will,
Make what laws you choose:
Yet there are high spaces of rapture
Which you can never touch;
They are beyond you and hidden from you.

We leave you to the dull assemblies,
Charades, cantatas, and lectures;
The civic meetings where you lie and act
And work up business;
The teas of forced conversation
And receptions of how-de-do's
And stereotyped smiles;
The church sociables;
And the calls your young men of clammy hands
And fetid breath
Pay to anaemic virgins:
These are yours,
Take them—

But I tell you,
In places you know not of,
We, the free spirits, the livers,
Guests at the wedding feast of life,
Drinkers of the wine made by Jesus,
Worshippers of fire and of God,
Who made the grape
And filled the veins of his legitimate children
With ethereal flame—
We the lovers of life in unknown places

Shall taste of ancient wine,
And put flowers in golden vases,
And open precious books of song,
And look upon dreaming Buddhas,
And marble masks of genius.
We shall hear the sound of stringed instruments
Voicing the dreams of great spirits.
We shall know the rapture of kisses
And long embraces,
And the sting of folly.
We shall entwine our arms in voluptuous sleep....
And in the misery of your denials,
And your cowardice and your fears,
You shall not even dream that we exist.

Unintelligible weeds! We, the blossoms of life's garden,
Flourish on the hills of variable winds —
We perish, but you never live.

# THYAMIS

Thyamis, a gallant of Memphis,
Where melons were served
Iced with snow from the Mountains of the Moon—
Thyamis, a philanderer in Alexandris
Rich in parchments and terebinth—
Lies here in the museum.
His lips are brown as peach leather,
Through which his teeth stick,
White as squash seeds.

    \*    \*    \*    \*    \*

Knowing that he must die and leave her,
He slew the lovely Chariclea
Who sailed with him on the Nile
Under the moon of Egypt.
This is the body of Chariclea,
Undesiring the arms of Thyamis.
This is the remnant of Chariclea,
Wrapped in a gunny sack,
Rotted with gums and balsams.

    \*    \*    \*    \*    \*

As the sands of the desert are stirred
By the wind when the sun sets,
The open door of the museum
Lets in a breeze to shake
The cerements of Chariclea,
And the stray hairs on the forsaken head
Of Thyamis.

    \*    \*    \*    \*    \*

Of desire long dead;
Of a murder done in the days of Pharaoh;
Of Thyamis, dying, who took to death
The lovely Chariclea;
Of Chariclea, who shrank
From the love-death of Thyamis—of all this
Unknowing, the multitude passes.

  *  *  *  *  *

# I SHALL GO DOWN INTO THIS LAND

I shall go down into this land
Of the great Northwest:
This land of the free ordinance,
This land made free for the free
By the patriarchs.

  \*  \*  \*  \*  \*

Shall it be Michigan,
Or Illinois,
Or Indiana?
These are my people,
These are my lovers, my friends—
Mingle my dust with theirs,
Ye sacred powers!

  \*  \*  \*  \*  \*

Clouds, like convoys on infinite missions,
Bound for infinite harbors,
Float over the length of this land.
And in the centuries to come
The rocks and trees of this land will turn,
These fields and hills will turn
Under unending convoys of clouds—
O ye clouds!
Drench my dust and mingle it
With the dust of the pioneers;
My mates, my friends,
Toilers and sufferers,
Builders and dreamers,
Lovers of freedom.

  \*  \*  \*  \*  \*

O Earth that looks into space,
As a man in sleep looks up,
And is voiceless, at peace,
Divining the secret—
I shall know the secret
When I go down into this land
Of the great Northwest!

    \*    \*    \*    \*    \*

Draw my dust
With the dust of my beloved
Into the substance of a great rock
Upon whose point a planet flames,
Nightly, in a thrilling moment
Of divine revelation
Through endless time!

# THE HOUSE ON THE HILL

Eagle, your broken wings are tangled
Among the mountain ferns
Upon a ledge of rock on high.
Below, the yawning chasm turns
To blackness, but the evening planet burns
Above the gulf in a gold and purple sky!

Vultures and kites
Fly to their rookeries
In the rocks
With swift and ragged wings against the lights.
From levels and from leas
Hasten the returning flocks.
Foxes have holes and serpents the grass for flight.
Eagle, arise! It is night.

The world's wanderer finds you
As he climbs the mountains
In the unending quest.
Can you spread your wings across the darkening chasm
To that craggy nest,
Where the foreboding mate lies still?
Croak for the evening star,
And beat your shattered wings against your breast!
Across the gulf, the wanderer sees afar
A light in the house on the hill!

from
*The Open Sea*

(1921)

# ULYSSES

Settled to evenings before the doorway
With Telemachus, who sat at his knee:
"Why did you stay so long from Ithaca,
Leaving my mother Penelope?"

The eyes of the hero rolled and wandered,
Thinking of Scylla and Sicily.
"That's a hard question," answered Ulysses,
"Harder, if answered, for you to see.

"There was the Cyclops, there was Aeolus,
There were the Sirens, and Hades for me;
Apollo's oxen, Hades' horrors,
Circe, and then Ogygia.

"All these after the war, Telemachus—
Too long a tale, as you will agree.
The bards must write it: when you are older,
Read till the gray hairs give you the key

"Of the wonder and richness that were your father's
Life in the war, the long way home.
No man has lived as I, Telemachus;
None ever will live, in the days to come,

"A life that followed the paths and hollows
Of Time, the wayward ways of the streams
That flow round earth, the winds and waters
Of passion, wisdom, thought, and dreams.

"There are two things, my boy, and only
Two in the world, remember this:
One thing is men, the other women;
And after the two of them, nothing is.

"I have known men as kings and warriors,
Known them as liegemen, spears of the line.
Good enough lamps for workaday darkness—
But they are not food, they are not wine;

"They are not heat that stirs the secret
Core of the seed of a man, be sure.
And I, Ulysses, needed the planets
And suns of the spring to live, to mature."

"What do you mean?" asked Telemachus,
"And say, is it true you lost eight years
Away from Ithaca, me, and my mother,
Because of a certain Calypso's tears?"

The eyes of the hero rolled and wandered.
"There now, my boy, you have the truth.
I'll try to tell you; perhaps you'll get it
In spite of your filial love, and your youth.

"First, understand there are two things only:
One is women, the other men.
And men I knew, before and at Troyland,
And searched their hearts again and again.

"What do you get? Secrets of cunning,
Cruelty, strength: much that you use
In the battle with them; but what's a woman?
She is the mother, she is the Muse

"That leads and lifts to life—Telemachus,
How can I tell you?—have a care!
Young men seize on the words of wisdom,
And find their hands in a silken snare:

"Hearing blindly, seeing literally,
What is a sword, a lamp, a shield.
Touch and learn: the name is only
The shell wherein the thing is concealed."

"What do you mean?" asked Telemachus.
"What do I mean? Attend to me!
I'll try to tell you, telling a story
Of the island called Ogygia.

"I know women—how shall I tell you?
Women are good, and good is wine.
Yet how to tell the wine, and the women
Who turn their adorers into swine.

"You must have the aid of Hermes, swiftness
Of spirit and sense, to tell them apart;
How to be strong, how to be tender,
How to surrender, yet keep your heart.

"Easy for me to baffle Circe,
Easy the Sirens to slip—just wax!
I steered for Ithaca, you, and your mother,
Isle to isle on the ocean's tracks,

"Until I came and saw Calypso....
Son, you would be with Calypso yet!
It takes a hero suppled in flame
To see Calypso and leave; forget

That face and voice enough to leave her,
Spurn her promises, turn from her tears,
And come to Ithaca with this doorway,
Age that hovers, the little years."

"What do you mean?" asked Telemachus.
"Live and learn," Ulysses replied.
"Calypso promised me youth eternal
If I would stay and make her my bride."

"And why not stay?" asked Telemachus,
"To have her for wife, if not a youth
Eternal given you?" "Boy of me, listen
Now for the core of the deepest truth:

"We dined in grottoes of blooming ivy;
We supped in halls of cedar and gold.
We slept on balconies, sapphire-tented—
But even this, I found, grew old.

"I saw her beauty bare by starlight,
And by the sea in the sun, and stoled
In silk as white as snow on Parnassus—
But even this, I found, grew old.

"Her tresses smelt of the blooms of Hymettus,
Her breasts were cymbals sweet to behold;
Her voice was a harp of pearl and silver—
But even this, I found, grew old.

"Her lips were like the flame of a taper
Scented and musical, as she would fold
White arms over the brawn of my shoulders—
But even this, I found, grew old.

"She promised me this and youth forever,
So long as the sun and the planets rolled.
I knew they were gifts she could not give me:
Empty promises too grow old.

"And even if given, why forever
Live the things that have grown enough?
She loved me, wonderful Calypso.
But what is love? It is only love.

"And the salt of a man turns to his doorway;
He makes his will for his blood at the end.
My boy, that's why I left Calypso
And came to you. Do you comprehend?

"To sit unshorn, and clothed as I choose,
Talk with the swineherd, potter or shirk;
To babble at ease, my boy, with your mother—
Around the house, at rest or at work.

"And you must not forget, Telemachus,
In order to have immortality
It had to be with Calypso! Therefore
I came to you and Penelope,

"Who soon will leave me, at best, or else
I'll leave you for the Isles of the Blest.
I find this doorway good, Telemachus,
As a place to dream and a place to rest."

"I do not understand, Ulysses,
Father of me. At first the call
Of the blood, I thought, would hasten you homeward.
And now I wonder you came at all

"Here to Ithaca. What, my father,
Is here but my mother, growing old,
Aged Laertes, and me your son—
What of Calypso's hair of gold?

"What of the island, what of the feasting,
What of her kisses? Were it I,
I'd spurn eternal youth; as a mortal
Live with Calypso until I should die."

"I have no doubt," said the many-minded
Great Ulysses. "It's plain to see
You are a boy yet. When is supper?
Go ask your mother Penelope."

from
*The New Spoon River*

(1924)

## MARX THE SIGN PAINTER

When Spoon River became a ganglion
For the monster brain Chicago,
These were the signs I painted, which showed
What ruled America:
Vote for Patrick Kelly and save taxes;
I am for men, and this is the cigar;
This generation shall not see death;
Hear Pastor Valentine;
Eat Healthina and live;
Chew Floss's gum and keep your teeth;
Twenty-five dollars for a complete funeral;
Insure your life;
Three per cent. for your money;
Come to the automat.
And if there is any evidence
Of a civilization better,
I'd like to see the signs.

## YET SING LOW

Yee Bow was killed by the son of Rev. Wiley,
And they wound his pigtail around his head
And buried him near Chase Henry.
No laundry for me,
But the Golden Pheasant
Where I served steak as well as chop suey,
And I wore their clothes and cut my cue,
And read the magazines and the dailies,
No longer a Chinese heathen.
But did I forget my City of Flowers?
No! For I lighted my pipe and dreamed:
And the water spouts on Bindle's Block
Were twisted dolphins on temple roofs;
Ash barrels in the alley became
Buddhas in bronze by an ivied wall;
The water tower seemed like a pagoda
At Ta-Li Fu; and the lilac bushes
Spread into courtyards full of blossoms.
Ding! went the register, Boom! went the drum,
As the Salvation Army passed and shouted
The blood of the Lamb . . . but I heard the bells
And gongs of Buddha on high, far away,
Where a poppy moon hangs over the hills
As yellow as moth wings, under a sky
As white as the shrines or the glistening streams
In the Valley of Fragrant Springs!

## HENRY ZOLL THE MILLER

Have you ever noticed the mill pond in the dog days?
How it breeds wriggling life,
And seethes and crackles with poisonous froth,
Then lies as still as a snake gone blind?
And how can the mill pond know itself
When its water has caked to scum and worms?
And how can it know the world or the sky
When it has no mirror with which to see them?
But the river above the bend is wise:
Its waters are swift and cold and clear,
Always changing and always fresh,
And full of ripples and swirls and waves
That image a thousand stars by night,
And a thousand phases of sun and clouds,
By a changing movie of forests and hills!
And down in its healthful depths the pickerel
Chase each other like silver shadows,
And the swift game fish swim up the stream.
Well, this is the soul of a man, my friend:
You brood at first, then froth with regret,
Then cake with hatred and sink to dullness;
Or else you struggle and keep on the move,
Forget and solve and learn and emerge
Full of sparkle and stars.
And down in your depths there's flashing laughter,
Swimming against the current!

# THE TOMBS OF THE GOVERNORS

*Forgotten Governors*
We are the forgotten rulers.
We have left no story
Of our great friends who maneuvered us into office,
And stood behind the throne after we were in.
Some of us waved the bloody shirt and were elected—
Some of us were elected
Because our fathers were able wavers of the bloody shirt.
All of us were creatures of interests,
Little beliefs, empty programs,
Deceiving promises.
Living for nothing, we left nothing.
Our memories died with the deaths
Of our patrons and protégés,
And those who attended the New Years' parties
At the executive mansion.


*Abraham Lincoln Pugsley*
I worked my way through business college,
And received the degree of M.A.—
Master of Accounts.
I taught school and studied law at night.
I became a judge of election, then precinct captain,
Then a committeeman with a string of delegates,
Then master of a district; all the while practicing law.
I forced my nomination for state's attorney,
Helped by the reform newspapers, and was elected.
Instead of taking bribes from saloon keepers and gamblers,
As my predecessor did,
I prosecuted them, and multiplied the prosecutions,
Forcing them to plead guilty—and I grabbed the fines,
And became rich on fines.
I was powerful now, and forced my nomination for governor.
I entered the executive office empty-headed, but befriended
By the powers that fight saloon keepers and gamblers,
And the labor unions.
Traditions, liberties, philosophies

Were nothing to me.
I even tried for a third term,
But I saw the storm coming, and slipped into the cellar
Of private life.
Around me are the graves of the soldiers
Killed in a strike that I crushed—
I was a governor of the state!


*Elliott Hawkins Hammond*
No pioneer, nor the son of one—
A lawyer's son, and a college man,
A real sophisticate from the start,
A twentieth century product.
I took my cue from Lambert Hutchins,
Who sold his vote in the legislature
To the railroad that wanted the water front
There in Chicago—but I was a "Packard,"
Where he was only a democrat wagon:
I headed a legislative committee
Commissioned to decide the titles
To lands submerged on the water-front.
And thus, instead of having a purse
Slipped to me for a favoring vote,
I edged along, and edged along,
And pecked away at the giant Theft,
Until it was almost ready to fall.
Well, who could shore it up but me?
So I shored it up, for contributions:
Ten thousand here, ten thousand there.
Then the war came on! And I plunged in,
And risked my life for the sacred cause
Of the world made safe for democracy.
When I came back, a grateful people
Elected me their governor!

## FRANK BLATT

Here I lie, rotted down from two hundred pounds of flesh
To less than a pound of mud.
After eating four hundred steers,
And two thousand bushels of corn,
And ten thousand loaves of bread,
And drinking five thousand gallons of whiskey.
What for? To give me strength to blat,
So that I could buy beef and bread and whiskey,
And blat!

## MRS. FRANK BLATT

Where would my mother and my sisters have been buried,
Not to speak of myself,
If I had not married Frank Blatt. . . .
I the stenographer, fat and a little old?
And at what board would my mother and sisters
Have fed,
If I had not captured him and he had not taken them in,
There to that household of the full larder
And the mortgaged roof?
Here we are then, lying around Frank Blatt:
We the Blatts, and my mother and sisters the Wallups!
Passing from corn and beef
To the bread which whoso eats, lives forever!

## HORACE KNIGHT

Friends! Shall your White Houses and executive mansions,
Your halls of the States and the Republic,
Be occupied by the thin-lipped and the bald-headed?
By the graduates of business colleges,
The readers of subscription books,
The fanatics on economies,
The hunters of vice and crime,
The wearers of hand-me-down Prince Alberts
And satin-stuffed ties,
The interpreters of democracy as mediocrity?
Or shall the lovers, the livers,
The well sexed, the philosophers, the artists,
The viewers of life as Freedom and Beauty,
Occupy your White Houses and executive mansions,
And have something to say about the Republic
Founded by Tom Paine and Ben Franklin
And Thomas Jefferson,
And the other bully begetters of children,
And of ideas: who knew the difference between a Rembrandt
And a chromo,
Between grape juice and Madeira;
And who knew that friendship and hospitality and happiness
Are worth all the principles and preachments in the world?

## JOSEPH RUHE

Urged by the wisdom
That the dead wish to speak to the living
More than the living wish to speak to the dead,
And have more to tell the living
Than the living have to tell the dead,
I worked at my psychoradiograph
Amid the smiles of Spoon River.
And now that I am here, I would tell you
The secret of love and music,
And the sorrow of hills, and vanished days,
And what it is that breaks your hearts
With music and love,
While making you sing and love!

# ROLAND FARLEY

Brooding light which saw not, and yet saw
What eyes saw not that needed light to see.
And thought which was all eyes, and made of life
Sound, and of inner light made thought and song.
Sight sphered in darkness, even as an urn which shuts
From the soul's candle winds of the lawless dark,
And leaves the soul's dreams burning in a calm
As a star hidden in the bowl of night....
What one of you, Spoon River, grieved for me;
Rejoiced not in my gift for light denied;
Saw not my heaven for my sunset sea,
Nor knew my heaven and my sea were one—
One splendor and one secret sensed afar?
That light and thought and sound are one in some
Sphere where no eyes are, and no need of eyes!

# JACK KELSO

To rear, to watch, to lose;
To be the soul of a sailor's wife: to wait.
To be a workman with adze and plane,
And to see your finished ship sail off,
And to know it no more.
To hear of the storms it weathered, the ports it reached.
To live here to the day of my death,
With the old things we had together, he and I:
The fiddle, the tramps by the river,
The rod and the gun,
And Shakespeare under a tree.
While he was commanding armies,
And wresting laws from mountains cloven asunder
By lightning and earthquakes,
To remain a fisherman and a fiddler—
But living days of wonder
About my storm-embattled chum,
And wondering if I ever knew him,
And if I were I!

## CONRAD HERRON

I wrote no book, Spoon River;
I left no library to you;
I endowed no school for you;
My face is not embossed in bronze
In the court-house corridor
As the faces are of Editor Whedon,
And Thomas Rhodes the banker.
But did I do nothing for you,
Did I leave you no legacy?
Is it worth nothing to you
That, dying with cancer,
I endured with fortitude and patience?

## THOMAS NELSON

There were two supreme moments in my life:
First when, amid applause,
I ascended the platform of power
As president of the county board.
Second, when I sat alone, ill, half speechless,
In an ante-room, before the beginning
Of my successor's inaugural.
And there, in that moment of passing out,
To have Henry Cabanis,
Who had fought me all my term,
And defeated my plan for good roads
Connecting the townships—
To have him appear at the door,
Brisk as a dwarf, glittering with victorious malice,
Notched and elfin as a frosted oak leaf,
Bitter with nut gall…
To have him appear, and ask with bland contempt:
"Any final directions?"

from
*Selected Poems*

*(1925)*

# THE CORN

    I.

On the white skeletons of poplar trees,
Or fluttering to the tips of blasted reeds,
Or searching the wind-threshed floor for seeds,
The blackbirds swarm like bees.
And with roulades liquid as water tones
They sing to the sapphire pools of March's sky,
Till the air is full of swinging xylophones. . . .
Their wings are starred with fire,
Gules of a heraldry that trumpets May,
When every slope and valley of vine and brier
Will hang like mists of moss, or the sea's spray.
Verdure upon the pastures will be drawn
In flames of green, spreading afar like dawn.
Meanwhile the yellow hills will drowse
Like lions on the meadow's floor,
And through their manes the rushing winds will pour,
Making great billows where the cattle browse
And racing the shadows of clouds
Over the sliding plain,
And blowing new greens out of the fluttering shrouds
Of flags and stalks, and throbbing the bandaged vein
Of earth where frost serrates the stream;
Till the brown quietudes of the fields get rain,
And stir, yet sleep to dream
Of the corn, the emerald parallels of the corn
That run from the hills line after line,
As fine as grass is fine. . . .
This is the birth of the corn, the corn!

    II.

  The wreck of the Indian villages,
  The stocks and shocks that stand
    After the ruinous rains and the pillages
    Of the palefaced snow that conquered the land.
These must be broken, swept away and burned
    To give this soil, this Ethiop breast
    To the nursing lips of the corn.

And at night when the wind has turned
To the south, and out of the odorous darkness, like an enchanter's
      horn,
    Breathes the desire of the hills, the earth's unrest,
    Bringing near and bearing afar
The staccato croak and guttural gurgle of frogs;
Then the windrows flutter with flames, with shadows shaken
By the breeze's blankets, the signals of war
Waged for the land, for the frost-forsaken
Soil of the corn, the heron-flight of the fogs!
    So the way is made for the share,
    Which buries the meteor dazzle of the sun
Under the long uncoiling rhythm of the loam;
Strip after strip for the teeth of the harrow to tear,
    Until there are miles of garden won
    For the corn to come:
For the spiral whorl of the disk that rakes and hoes,
And the clocklike tick of the planter timing the rows
From gossamer dawn till the western windows gleam
With the candle of evening, the planet of spring.
All day through, as the heavens teem
With the meadow lark, that flies the imps of the breeze
Who leave their frolic among the fennel and grasses
To puff his wings and blow his feathers
Amid the crannies of light, the blue crevasses,
The peaks of gold where his heart upgathers
Strength for song to the cloud as it passes.

      III.
    Silent slide of the river,
    As the corn grows
    In the June whose gold and purples quiver:
    June of the lilac and rose,
    As the leaves of the corn unclose,
Furl at evening, flutter in the morning,
Lie becalmed, stretched to the heat of June
Voluptuously at noon,
While the sun is silently adorning
Out of his fiery hair the spikelets of the tassels,
Out of his heart of flame the grains of sweetness.
Every stalk is like a tall bandmaster,
With panicled cap and staff of the glistening blade,

Globed with a mimic sun whose splendor dazzles
The lower leaves that move like the marching of feet,
As the sun god beats the music faster
Amid the interlacing lances of light and shade.
    This is the sun dance, dance of the Sioux,
      Singing, come down, come down!
Come down, O Fire, from your space between the tents of heaven:
Camp fire of the Great Spirit, come and imbue
The fattening ears with fiery leaven,
Strength for the country and the town!
Pour on us blinding light,
And close our eyes that we may dream
Of men and cities, great prosperities
Of states, of ships that bless the seas,
Of temples of renewed nobilities
Built to your Amphion music with our might!
Help us to close, renew, redeem.
Come down, that we may use the food
Which the little folk of the soil prepared for us;
That the cycle of our servitude
To flocks that wait, yet fared for us,
And man whose toil and fortitude
Saw all and wisely cared for us,
May give him strength to struggle and reveal
The world of soul, as he has drawn the world
Of grinding stones, the kettle and the bin,
To the steam-driven mill, the storing tower of steel.

    IV.
    1.
July over the corn!
July, of the lavender slate-sloped west of noon!
July, of the boundless miles of shimmering quiet,
The white heat concentration
Of the corn's rapt reverie and castle-building,
And dreams of the harvest coming soon.
July, of the corn's long tongues whose diet
Is taken out of the vacuoles of torrents of splendor
And changed to wine and honey, oil and gilding
For the swelling grains in pockets tied with silk
And lined with satin white as milk:
Gold to be for man, the spender.

July, of the golden pollen sifting,
Dried and driven by winds shifting,
Bringing lightning, rain, and hail,
Before the deep roots fail.
July, when the crow with open beak
Pants for breath in the tree by the river,
Where purple lights over the rushes quiver,
And the water snake, a ribbon of yellow and red,
Is coiled on the upturned crust of the creek.
July of the deep sea shadows between the rows,
Wherein no light is shed
Save phosphors, and the arrow-glint
Thrown as an Indian an arrow throws!
July, when the still, hot hedges blossom with mint
And the thirsty ironweed droops its head,
And no sound stirs the mystery of this birth
Wrought by the earth and the sun her lover,
This breathless breath of the mating sun and earth—
Save the far-borne clang of the mower amid the clover
As it climbs the swale to the horses' tread. . . .

    2.

Stillness! Save as the sun moves onward to the south,
And by unseen degrees brings August days,
When little blue mists rise around the stalks
In dawns of drenching dews that wet the drouth.
Save as summer-silenced crows, Mohawks
Of the garnered fields, come forth to glut
Their craws, and flying flake the sky
As with the sick corn's wind-unloosened smut!
Stillness! Save for the coming of September's haze,
When the quails call, and ecstatic jays
Rejoice to see their wings stained with the dye
Of steel-blue heavens, and scream out the cool
Colors of the Autumn-filtered pool!
And save as seed birds chirp among dry weeds,
Or troops of sparrows seek the bursting pod
For glistening seeds;
Or the belated bee hums round the goldenrod,
Or blooms of fall, where the sumach bleeds.
And save as, later, among the surrendering ears
The huskers and the gatherers call,

Plucking the nuggets of gold, the magical
Smeltings of the sun, ere the frost sears.

    V.
    1.

This is America, this the Indian maize,
The Maya symbol of the power of man:
The growth that is American,
The ruler of our hopes and days.
This is the land most rich, this Illinois,
In the corn that started with the yield
Of the Indian patch, food for a little clan,
And widened to the thousand-acred fields
Around Aurora, Lincoln, and Amboy,
Over the broad, tilled levels of McLean,
Logan, Menard and Fulton, Sangamon,
Where round the soil the fertile rivers run.
This, the beginning of the sovereign reign
Of coal and steel, the mile-long train,
Freighters and the gray slim shadows of the lakes,
The clicker and the Dorian-columned room
Where coins and magic hieroglyphs
Symbol the corn once scrawled on caves.
This soul awakened is the soul which makes
The Nation's soul, and wrecks or slays or saves;
Becomes the spirit of progress, or enslaves
The spirit of man in freighters and storing cliffs
Where it remains, as in a desert land,
The sport of devils haunting the shimmering sand!

    2.

Come down, O Sun, to the corn; reveal
Souls vast as the driven mill, the bins of steel.
Help man to grow, the spiritual
Famine of his faith forestall,
And by that prosperous settlement unseal
Wisdom and visions of undreamed-of weal,
Mites of the earth for corn, and corn for cattle,
Cattle for man, and in the cyclic strength
Brought down from you, O Sun, to earth, the breast
Of all maternities: first for might in battle—
As when the corn-fed youth of all the length

Of Illinois stormed Vicksburg's deadly crest—
And next for the balanced use of wealth;
For all that gives the race to health;
For leisure and, through leisure, Beauty, Truth;
For Love, the soul of fire;
And Wisdom, soul of light;
So that this land, that never had a youth
But in a rude routine of gold desire
Has crawled the ground, might suddenly mutate
By long-stored life and might,
And blossom with a blossom never known,
Evolving the soul of man, which has outgrown
The repetitions of material Fate!

## WORLDS

I have known or seen all the worlds of this world,
And some of the worlds of the world to come;
And I say to you that every world lives to itself
And is known to itself alone,
Though it moves among the other worlds of this world.

I was in the hospital and given up to die—
And that is one of the worlds.
I had turned blue,
And they moved me to the charity ward of the dying—
And that is one of the worlds.
They had screens around us,
So that we could not see each other die.
But they had no way to shut out from each of us
The cries and prayers of the others.
Next me was a little woman they called "Butterball"—
She was yellow from cancer,
And had been cut to death by the surgeons.
She cried all night; she died at dawn,
Just as I began to mend.

There is the world of the interns making love to the nurses.
And the world of the surgeons hurrying to dinners,
And the applause of learned societies.
And the world with their children at school, or in play,
Ignorant of what it means to be learned and notable,
And to be the children of such men.
There is the world of the policeman
Who walks by the hospital at night.
And the world of the taxi drivers
Who never see the hospital as they rush past.
There is the world of the man and woman in the taxi,
Kissing each other in anticipation of the place of assignation.
There is the world of the train crew
Who make up the limited back of the hospital;
And the world of travelers, happy or anxious,
Going or coming.
And this day, there was for myself

The world of getting well,
With its meaning and its happiness
Unguessed by the world of the well.
And my eyes were opened to the worlds
By suffering, and by coming from that world
Of the charity ward of the dying.
And I saw that there is the world of a merchant;
And the world of a judge;
And the world of a legislator, or a president;
And the world of a rich man;
And the world of a poor man;
And the world of a defeated man;
And the world of a victorious man;
And the world of a ruling nation;
And the world of a people who are ruled;
And the world of a servant, a laborer;
And the world of a master, and a user;
And the world of passion;
And the world of love;
And the world of envy;
And the world of hate;
And the world of strife;
And the world of convicts,
And those condemned to death.
And the world of war and warriors;
And the world of the young;
And the world of the old;
And the world of desire unceasing;
And the world of desire that is dead;
And the world of those who see God,
And the world of those who see Him not;
And the world of the faithful, the hopeful;
And the world of the doubters and the hopeless.
And the world of those who have loneliness forever;
And the world of those who ease loneliness
With futile activity;
And the world of those who seek truth and find it not;
And the world of those who never give up
In the search for beauty.
And the world of those to whom the world is harmonious sound.
And the world of those to whom the world is atoms or stars.
And the world of those to whom the world is a machine;

And the world of those to whom the world is life.
And the world of those to whom the world is an infinite mass
To be carved as the will wills;
And the world of those to whom the world is chaos;
And the world of those to whom the world is memory;
And the world of those to whom the world is regret;
And the world of those entangled in subtle horrors
And eaten minute by minute by thoughts that die not;
And the world of those who front and touch
The mystery of closing and suffocating horizons,
And the beleaguering Infinite
With brows of sentinel and arméd thought,
Standing at the heights and the Thermopylae of life,
Even to the hour of surprise from the plains
By Death, the Persian. . . .

And I saw that every soul is a world to itself,
Making its own murmurous music night and day,
And having its realest world in itself,
And knowing none of the other worlds.

And what worlds beyond our world
Know our world of worlds?
All worlds of this world, and all worlds,
May be but the world of the mind of God,
Of which He is not conscious Himself
Unless He chooses to think of them.

from
*Lichee Nuts*

(1930)

## ON CONTENTMENT

First wife dead, second wife gone to China.
No children, no house, only this little room:
This stove, couch, bowl and spoon and image of Buddha.
But a little silver laid away, and food enough;
Mind at rest, or filled with good thoughts,
And long talks with Yang Chung every day.

## YET WEI AT THE THALIA THEATRE

Yet Wei smokes a pipe sometimes,
Then goes to Thalia theater:
Not to see Chinese play
But to hear the lonely music of Chinese orchestra,
Which sounds like hills, like the desert, like the plain,
Like stars, like moonlight, like summer sky and still river.
For then, he says, he sees coming out of the music
The moats of the Great Wall full of lotuses;
Then he sees green lands, and windblown willows,
And the blossoming valleys of the Yangtse-kiang;
Then he sees the shaded grays of earth and sky
Tinged with blue and rose;
Then he sees the tomb of the Ming emperor
Amid temples and palaces, and the carved figures
Of harnessed elephants and horses,
And snarling tigers and lions.
But when the dream is brightest, and the music sweetest,
Saddest, and from the farthest distances calling,
Yet Wei says he floats over the long way to Tibet,
To Turkestan, to India,
Where the Himalayas fill the air
With a dumbness that will not let their music speak.
Then he passes across the Gobi desert,
And the Great Plain, where demons lurk
And wild winds cry
Vastness and solitude and eternal loneliness forever.
Then, says Yet Wei, he sinks into a deeper dream,
And tears run down his cheeks.
For he sees thousands of years stretched like caravans,
He sees thousands of years of patient Chinese
Taking the burdened camels to India and Persia.

## FULL MOON ON THE BOWERY

The same evening Harry Chin saw blackbird
He took long walk through Bowery,
And under elevated as far as Rivington,
Then back to Mulberry,
Then down Broadway to City Hall Square.
The full moon rolled off the roofs of hot tenements,
Hung beside the nodding tower
Of the Woolworth building
Where blazing windows blinded the sky—
Till the moon looked like a wilted Nelumbian Lotus
In the hands of Hua Hsien,
The goddess of flowers, when she stands
By the shore of Hangchou.
Then Harry Chin, stepping amid
The tangle of steel and the rabble racket,
Thought of the night wind over Hangchou,
Which heaps the spun glass of sea foam
Against the reeds with the sound of blown frost
Where the naked moon bathes alone
With streaming hair.

# SAVING TEARS

Yuan Chang ask Yet Wei
Why he shed no more tears.
Yet Wei say:
"Saving tears for urine."

## ORIGIN OF SIN

Wah Tom say he know all about sin,
And Puritan, and being good in America.
How you mean? ask Hi Ho.
Well, say Wah Tom,
God put sex nerve in lips just for kiss,
Nothing else.
Along come devil and move nerve
To wrong place:
And that make shame, sin, Puritan,
Prohibitionist, law and order man—
All troubles.

# THE DEATH OF HIP LUNG

On the day of his death, Hip Lung arose
And dressed himself, and entered his store.
He took a jade Buddha and set it before him.
He lighted incense, opened his chest,
And chose from his treasures a vase of nephrite,
Feasting his eyes on the artist's work.
With voluptuous calm, he ran his fingers
Over the carvings of leaves and flowers.
Yet Wei watched him through the window,
Then went his way, and then returned:
There sat Hip Lung with the vase of nephrite
Folded about with his cold dead hands.

# THE DEPARTURE OF YET WEI

A few days after Hip Lung died,
Yet Wei prepared to go away.
To all who asked him where he was going,
He answered that he did not know.
"I shall cross the ferry to Jersey City," he said,
"And climb to the highest hill there,
In order to look for the last upon the towers of New York—
After that I shall wander."
And when he was ready to go,
Tuck High, Yuan Chang, Hi Ho,
And some others went with Yet Wei to the ferry.
Yet Wei got on the ferry weeping,
And all his friends wept.
Then Yet Wei gave a poem to Yuan Chang
To be read when they got back to Mott Street.
The capstans rattled, the chains clanked,
And with a whistle the ferry started.
Yet Wei gave one look and disappeared.
His friends watched the ferry
Till it was lost in the mists of the Hudson.

## YET WEI'S POEM

I went to his room: I saw his chest.
I took out his vase; I looked at it long.
I looked at the bronze jar with his ashes.
On a shelf was his pipe, on a stand his hat—
Everything said, "Hip Lung is gone."
Where shall I wander? There is no searching
Ever shall find him, yet wander I must.
Trains roar and rattle, peddlers are calling,
Children are playing, merchants talk.
Between the high buildings a strip of heaven
So empty, so blue, is a dragon's mouth
That gnaws at my heart and draws its life out;
While Something calls me, on high, far away.
This is the city of stone and iron
Whose pavements are vampire bones petrified,
Sapping the life of the children of labor
And giving nothing of life in return.
The Sun-Set Land of the Purple Hills
Calls me now, and I wander forth
With an empty heart once full and happy
For the love of Hip Lung, forever gone.

from
*Invisible Landscapes*

(1935)

## INVOCATION

Hertha, Rhea, Earth,
Mother, however named
Goddess of corn and birth
With wonder flamed:
As a mother who sends her son with a sword
To war for the land and the race,
You raise up men to follow your word,
And to dream of your face.

As a mother who stands at the open door
To greet the returning son
When the war is over,
So you take back to your breast again,
O mother and lover,
The life-worn children of men.

As the husks of weary blossoms
That are dried as wisps
On the tips of wooden stalks
By the foot-worn walks,
Our souls turn scale and lisp
With thought grown clear as horn,
Close-pressed to the brow's dry skin
With thinking worn;
With nothing at last between
Thought and the things of sight,
Save those calyces withered of life,
Transparent as light.

Feeling and thought have surged
To the petals' tips and rims;
They have vanished there and immerged
With light that no more limns.

Then you, O mother, seeing
Your sons from your life reduced,
In a secret under-breath
Say, "I am love and dreams;

Be at one again with my being,
Be genius again with me
As the core of life in the seed,
In blossom again to be freed.
Enter the soil and the streams,
Again with my current be blent
In my magnet element,
My spirit immanent."

## INVISIBLE LANDSCAPES

Dead flesh of men goes under
The landscape, and is sealed.
Their souls remain a wonder
Made one with hill and field,
And lie transparent shadows:
Like auras, or the light
Around eclipses, on meadows
Perceived by second-sight.
Each generation films
Its landscape, as the leaves
From stricken oaks and elms
Lay humus which Earth receives.
Each generation rises
From Earth and floats away—
But there's a soul that prizes
The Earth, and will not stray
From hills and plains unchanged,
Which moulded as it merged,
And never grows estranged,
And never is diverged.
That soul stays in the land;
It keeps the landscape true
To men who toiled and planned
Their days of living through.
That soul may be divined
With one's terraqueous eye,
Or felt as solar wind
Suddenly from the sky
Blown over pastures lying
Beyond the woodland's rim,
Which speaks of Nature crying
Her wound from shadows dim.

Like lights of afternoon
The invisible landscape shifts,
Yet always with a rune
Which nestles, flies and drifts;
But, drifting, forever blown,

Still enters the visible land
As spiritual tree and stone,
As hill or river sand.
It is man's flesh and blood
Become the Earth to quire
The Voice whose quietude
Echoes Eternal Fire.

How else do visions rise
From Walnut, Wyanet,
Shabbona Grove, with sighs,
And longing moods beget?
How do old houses and docks
At Lacon, Hennepin,
Say these are timbers or rocks
But something lives within?
The life force in a man
Keeps moulding him afresh:
The landscape follows the plan
That shapes a life of flesh.
The mole-like souls of the dead
In blindness creep beneath
The Earth, but upward send
These dreams of living breath.

How else do Naperville,
Neponset and White Hall,
The muser of mysteries, thrill
With visions of La Salle,
Marquette and Joliet?
Save that the landscape is
A spirit that won't forget
Strown men or fallen leaves,
But walks amid the storms
To keep its contours made
True to the ancient forms
Which leaves and spirits laid
In layers on layers, placed
Conforming to Earth's breast:
That the landscape may be traced,
And the souls of men expressed.

When over Starved Rock you watch
The crows at evening fly,
Within your heart to match
Is a sky for that lonely sky.
Your longings, aches, and dreams
Come from the landscape's scar,
Where soldiers by these streams
Went hasting forth to war
And never returned again,
Except as leaves that fell
To feed the landscape's pain,
Unseen, inaudible.

At Havana, where catfish
Are caught by the river-side,
Like a long-forgotten wish
Or a hope unsatisfied,
Around you like a ghost
Something will brush your brows:
It's Shearer, the smiling host
Of the old-time Taylor House,
Dead now these forty years.
And you may motor along
The length of the land with ears
Made wild with wine and song,
Not knowing the little towns,
The rivers, hills, and creeks—

Yet your heart will turn a clown's,
That slows before it breaks,
Seeing a tumbled fence
Or a yard with a single pine,
Or a swinging door that laments,
Or washing flapping the line;
Or plows or planters left
To rust where no one heeds;
Or horses of care bereft,
Or graves amid pasture weeds.
The invisible landscape brushes
Your idle cheek as you speed:
For here, where sunlight hushes,
Is the place of a vanished breed,

Who loved and suffered and fell
As leaves, and entered the peace
Of the land, and became the spell
Of whispering wind in trees.

There are landscapes hidden and piled
One after the other forever:
That was one when evening smiled,
And one that dock by the river.
When the prairie moon dips and races
By hills as you speed in the train,
That's the drawing anear of faces
Who have sunk as leaves in the rain
And become the soul of the soil,
And the memory passed from mind,
But remaining a sorcery coil
And an unheard voice in the wind.

You cannot have millions of men
Who march, who harvest and plow,
Who grow and die as grain,
Who feast, who laugh, who bow
Their heads in churches in tears
For kindred gone into the Earth,
For broken and meaningless years,
For love, for labor, for dearth,
Save invisible landscapes rest
In layers like fallen leaves,
Whose voice is the wind from the West
Where the middle meadow grieves;
Whose voice is the frozen lips
Of Earth, which echo Space,
As Earth lies under eclipse—
But the shadow is that of a Face.

# HYMN TO THE EARTH

### I.
Men coming from the twilight of the senses,
Where they knew not themselves, nor what was round them
Save with an animal eye, were as wolves or lions
Whose instincts, grooved by the hand of the past,
Led them to shelter and food and meats, and these alone.
Even then those cave-men peopled Nature with beings,
And dreamed there was mind in sticks and stones,
In animals, plants, and the Earth-stuff.
So twinkled at first the divination
That in the beginning was Mind.

### II.
Then, as soon as the eyes of these ancients
Learned to guide their minds by the light of heaven,
They rejoiced in communion with Nature;
They blessed the Earth of crocus and blooming hyacinth
Mingled amid the Spring grass by the fountained hills
Whereon were feeding, as lives separate from themselves,
Cattle and sheep.
Then, gladdened by Earth, and deeming that Earth and Heaven
Were peopled with gods behind whom omnipresence,
Hidden in air, made life of chaos and night,
They called Nature Pan, the All; and gave him a body
Shaggy of coat, with the hoof and beard of a goat.
They dreamed that he uttered the various cries of the woodlands,
And the windy headlands where multitudinous voices
Range from the wastes of the sea.
They gave him a pipe of reeds wherewith to murmur
His wounded passion, and echo
The cries of larks and halcyons and eagles,
Which fly with mourning over the tides of Autumn,
Or scream above the crags amid the lightnings.

### III.

With adoration they called Earth a kindly spirit,
A goddess, the wife of Heaven, the mother
Of men and gods, and the watcher of hearths
Where bread was baked and children danced.
For they beheld Autumn when pods were bursting,
And tough-coated fruits adhered to rabbits,
And dandelions and thistles drifted,
And the toad-flax was pushing its box of fruit
Into the crannies along the wall of the garden;
When snails retired between stones for rest,
And frogs retreated to holes in the banks,
And wasps hid down in the cracks of trees,
And hedgehogs curled for sleep in burrows,
And snakes grew torpid and intertwined;
And the cattle and sheep were huddled in byres
And nothing was left of the leaves but ashes,
And the blushes of sleep, and the drowsy purple
Of grapes made drunk by the sun, when they sang
And danced and worshipped Earth.

### IV.

In the rhythm of life, the sleep that is Winter
Filled them with wonder when paleness lay
On valleys and hills.
When the mountain hare, the Arctic fox, and the ptarmigan
Became the color of snow in retreats of stillness;
When bulbs tucked tight their coats and hid from the winds;
And water-plants for warmth sank down to the bottoms
Of streams whose doors were bolted with the iron of ice.

### V.

When they saw the bursting scales of buds that were rested,
And the leaves in the buds unclosing their spiral twists;
When the worker bee flew to the willow katkins
To gather pollen and nectar for hungry cradles;
When snails awoke to the drip of the water-clock
In the garden wall as the frost began to flow;
And the gnats made a raft of eggs which soared as a plane,
Only to be snapped down by awakening fish;
When the frog made lungs of gills, and brought up eyes
From its inner brain by the grace of immanent life;

When butterflies fluttered in pairs from flowering thickets;
And eels found the rivers, deserting the vernal sea
Leveled with April's calmness and stippled with rain;
When larks returned to the meadows sprinkled with cowslips,
And flowers abounded as far as the steppes of Asia,
Gorgeous with tulips;
When the stickleback glued his wattles together again
And mounted the nest to fight the foes of the brood:
Then the drama of hunger and love and thought in Nature
Fed men's dreams of a Mind in Earth.

### VI.

Thereafter came the drowsy richness of Summer,
When the sun's reflections dazzled the hills with eyes
Like the burning eyes of lions,
And the breezes were soft and walked with trees for feet;
When the mystical harvest drew anear,
And the leaf of the cabbage became a butterfly's wings,
And the worms of the earth returned to the song of the lark,
And the fruits of the earth were made into passion and thought
And hope that sailed as a spider the depths of air.
It was then these first men sought communion with Nature;
It was then they drank the god to be one with the god,
And built them altars of fire to worship the All.

### VII.

For they dreamed of a Life that worked these miracles,
Which was not Earth, but in Earth as a separate spirit
Moving through Earth as a Mind and in fellowship
With the motion of matter, the force of fire, and making
The mind of man with the food of Earth by Mind.
For they questioned how will and vision were in the mind of man,
If the Earth was blind and moved without will;
And whence were will and thought if not from Earth?
Yet what was Earth but a leaf of the Universe,
Gifted with life and with mind?
And what but a tree was the Universe, with roots
Deep in the soil of some immaterial earth?
And what was the All but Life, sustaining stars
And the sun and Earth?
Earth where no deadness is, but all is motion!
Earth with an inner being for man's communion!

Earth mothering man by self-existent life!

### VIII.

These ancient men dreamed of an immanent soul,
In which Earth was bathed and given breath by a Mind
As great as the body of the Universe
Which sustained all infinitudes and enclosed them,
Together with all living things, and man as well,
With feelings and thoughts whose roots were yet in Earth;
Together with their frames creating space and time,
And dimension; and which divined a flickering
Across the boundaries of length and breadth and height
Which might be time or motion, or might turn to space again,
Being itself the reflection of something afar.
For earth to them was the stops and the strings of a Mind,
And sang as a pipe to an infinite breath.
And if these ancient men had seen an organ
With bellows driven by a dynamo
They would have known the music of such reed-pipes
Could not be played without the composer's score,
Which persisted in memory or on parchment
Even after the keys, the pedals, and the pipes
Had been made ashes and scattered to the winds.

### IX.

For they saw in Earth the beautiful that is the unknown,
And Nature as necessity,
And the death of man as Nature,
And mind as the blossom of sacred fields,
And temples the growth of Earth and the mind.
For Earth contained the thought of man, though locked
In rock and soil; becoming thought again
Through the mind of man communing with Earth.
Earth! with its various forms of life,
Itself but a part of that Life which draws
On the blood of the All, then feeds the heart of man.
Earth! which embraces man with fateful love
Yet holds him off, clasping him fast that he may not leave her;
And apart, that he may reach a higher life.
Earth! That fills him with longing for words
To express what he knows not, but feels too deeply.
Earth! The veil of the intelligence of Nature,

Which owes nothing to any external essence
But contains within itself, from the All, the chlorophyll
Which extracts life from the universe.
Earth! Whose seeming lifelessness is deeper life,
Whose seeming unconsciousness is profounder thought,
Being at the basis of thought.
Earth! Which says that Death shall never awe man
Beneath a green hill, over which a Gibraltar
Of chalk-cloud looms out of the unseen ranges
Far and eternal; nor in an orchard where summer
Moves the leaves and scissors leaves from the sky;
Nor in the thrilling quiet of midnight stars;
Nor in places of no sound, where Nature moves
Man's sense of oneness with her and of kinship,
And intimation that nothing is but Mind.

    X.

For they worshipped Earth, and felt the Universe
As rhythm wherein the mighty heaven imaged
The white fire nebulae of thought, whose strophes
Kept time with man's in moods of highest thought.
This was the Universe which a turtle's shell
Strung with the guts of a sheep: an instrument
Which still retained the life of Nature, sang
Through its remembrance of Nature the inner secrets
Of sheep and turtles, and scaled the lore of the sky,
And sang of fruitfulness when the sea-side vineyards
Piled with grapes the bowls of the hills,
And men made fire by the sea and adored the sun.
For these ancient men divined a mind in Earth
Made of the minds of men,
And of animals and plants immersed in the greater Mind,
Which were as senses, knowing or not knowing themselves,
But which reached out to know that greater Mind
Of which, as senses, they were listening tendrils.
These ancient men saw matter moved by force behind it,
And followed the orbit
Along which life vanishes into matter
And appears again by the marching laws of music.

### XI.

They caught the rhythm of the universe
Through the drip of rain-drops from a quiet leaf,
Or zephyrs puffing at a harebell;
And through the rhythm of meadows when the wind blows,
Or of wheat stalks leaning motionless at sunset;
And through the rhythm of nightfall when the sky closes
Like the lips of a tragic chorus;
Or the rhythm of snow on the mountains;
And of high, lonely places
Where Earth dreams as a mother nursing her child;
And the rhythm of fire and light, and of the heavens at night,
When to survey the breathless banks of stars
Reveals at last a wheeling, as when on a slope
The dandelions and white daisies stretch their hands exultingly,
Making the hillside race to its crest of green.

### XII.

Not by faith, but by the wide wandering of vision
Those ancient men perceived a world beyond this world,
Whereof this world was the shadow, eclipsing
That father world, which had a will
And was Mind below the beginning of Earth and life.
For in the lowest forms of living creatures
They saw the prophecy and preparation
Of what is highest, even without knowing
That all the series of lower life is traversed
In the developing embryo of man.
They saw life first as it sparkles in sea-jelly,
And as it burns in fungus till it lights
The candle in the cabin,
Though hidden from their vision was the cell
Which can be irritated and fatigued,
And when fatigued refuses to respond,
And thus refusing is the beginning of memory.
They saw the oneness of Nature without knowing
That all living things come from Earth's chemicals,
And without knowing the alchemy of the green leaves
Which pluck from sunlight
The food of animals and man, and make
Life-giving air for breath.
They saw the undulate medusae of swinging waves:

Great films of glue with patches of purple,
Of blue and orange, struck with the arrows of Eros
Wherefrom arose, from that sun-pregnant spoon-drift,
The adorable Aphrodite.
And in these primal forms of life
Which shrink from shock as if netted with nerves,
And respond to light and are an eye,
They found the sleeping mind of man.
They knew this, even though they knew not
How this stuff feeds and breeds and lives forever
And, as Earth's mind, has immortality;
Nor knew that Nature is tirelessly trying
And failing, and trying again,
And, having once succeeded, gifts with memory
The tree or lizard to follow the way of triumph.
Yet seeing life and mind in Earth, they knew
That mind could never rise from Earth unaided.

    XIII.
They would have rejoiced to know
That light is waves and bullets side by side;
That there are waves of energy too long
To touch respondingly the life-stuff of the sea.
Such would have tallied with their soul's exploring,
Guessing at secrets which form no intelligible thought,
Being the shadows of light, then the shadow of shadows,
And then an inane which gestures beyond space and time.

    \*    \*    \*    \*    \*

But as the leaf does not grow anxious,
Fearing that it must hold to its life as a leaf
Or death will come to the tree;
And as the twig rests in the friendship of the branches,
And the branches feed on the trunk
And the trunk on the roots,
And the roots on Earth, and Earth on the mind in the Earth—
So did these ancient men have peace
In seeing that what seemed separateness
Was one life in Nature, and was fed by one Life.
They saw that when man awoke and knew
That he was a man, as a leaf might know itself as a leaf
And dream that it was separate from the tree,

Then tragedy began. But they did not abandon
The quest of self-life, nor refuse to return to Nature.
Nor were they ever so submerged in self
That they forgot their vision of the All.
It was their tragedy, as ours, to find their spirits
Not fully manifested by their flesh. Some remnant
Of their life as thought remained in the mystic Earth
Toward which they toiled, as Plato toiled
To find the archetypes of existences.

### XIV.

We their children, we the more conscious leaves,
We with glasses and with mathematics,
And infinitesimal measurements and menstrums,
Dream the same dream, but with a clearer insight
See consciousness hiding itself in mystery;
And in far wandering moods, fitting the wheeling seasons,
Match with our minds the moods of Spring and Winter,
Summer and Autumn.
But from our subtle lenses still flies the secret;
All deeper delving in the realm of matter
Reveals an energy still further hidden,
And with a finer tenuousness dependent
On time, the phantom of mortality:
An energy more fertile in production,
Forever locked in landscapes and in stones.
This it is which invests a lonely field
With a presence more living as there is no sound
Around it, nor in the valley nor on the hill;
And which animates the summer clouds;
And guards with beings brooks and waterfalls;
And guides the rivers, and presides along
Old roadways by dilapidated barns;
And fills the awful forms of mountain tops
With powers as if such magnitude alone
Sufficed to speak the Earth-mind, which would speak
The Universe and wake perceiving ears.

### XV.

We, who have traced all Earth-stuff to electrons,
Leave to the children of the time to be
The exploration of this living inane

In which electrons, bodiless as Time,
At moments cling and hold the Earth together
And whirl as order and eternal beauty;
When Thought has magnified the mind for thinking
A thousandfold, as the aerial has extended
The single sense of hearing around the world.
Now to this generation, these electrons
Are only dots within a vitreous void.
As an eye becomes a Milky Way of motes
Under the microscope, so has the Eye
Lost its man-likeness under the gaze of science,
Even while science feels a Mind is staring
Into its eyes that search the vacancy,
The Pan it fancies is intelligence
Listing as air on Earth and through the gardens
Of nebulae that stir as feathered light.

  \*  \*  \*  \*  \*

Still, with these ancient men, we stand before
The Earth, embodiment of persisting life,
And as her children hymn her sacredness,
Our selves, which are to be of Earth again
In the eternal circuit of birth and death.

## THE GOD OF THE AILANTHUS

With stripped, laced boughs this old ailanthus tree,
Here in this court of city houses, shakes
Amid December's lights and winds, and wakes
All memories of the fleeting deity

Revealed as shining loneliness, which abides
For a moment only by bare portal vines
Whereon a glance of ghostly sunlight shines—
Then, being a presence, turns and hides.

It is the god! By him is now recalled,
Through this ailanthus tree, these phosphor beams,
Gray-terraced Taos where an Indian dreams
In a bleak corner, sitting still and shawled;

By him are dunes re-visioned, above which the blues
Of vaulted heavens pause; by him appear
Rushes wind-swept and river-reaches sere,
And seas in sudden silence by Santa Cruz;

And gulls that drift through wingéd mists, where tolls
The mournful buoy by dragon shores
Where foam is sunlit but no water roars,
So far away the tide is on the shoals.

When icicles burn with noons and drip,
And at the corner of the shed the hills
Are tranced, and where the witch-wind shrills,
There, half invisible, he baffles augurship.

By a dead crow's feathers of a sudden stirred,
By smoke whirled from chimneys, or a fluttering cloth
Hung by the door, or totems moving, wroth,
See! See! where he glides, by distance undeterred.

He, being daimon, demigod, or gnome,
Steals through the days, half-shown and half-revealed
And, kindred to the loneliness of the soul,
Lures the homeless, himself without a home.

## HOBOKEN FROM TWENTY-THIRD STREET


From Twenty-third and Seventh Avenue
The houses of old Hoboken, perched upon
The Jersey Palisades,
Look huddled against the yearning sky.
At the end of Twenty-third, the ferry sheds
The Jersey shore and the Hudson shuts from view,
Where endless ferries ply
From dusk to dawn.

Against the paling day,
Or when sun sets and the heaven glows,
There old Hoboken stands
Aloft, and peers into New York which flows
With multitudes and cars and noise:
As a traveler, pausing on his way,
Looks from a height around the lower lands.

In these houses of old Hoboken, there are youths
Who look across the Hudson River and dream
About New York, which soothes
The lust of adventure swimming against the stream.
They see the Woolworth Tower, the Empire Tower,
And ocean liners and freighters and ferry boats
Which, swan-like, hour by hour
Set forth. They see the fire-fly lights
Of the city, and on the river, and hear the notes
Of luring whistles when the night's
Darkness is on the Bay, and the sea draws
Dreams and tides
As the waters crawl and pause
Through which the liner slides.

But in New York, imaginative eyes
Look west on Twenty-third
At old Hoboken, seeing against the sky's
Mysterious emptiness
The memory of lands which gird
These houses of the Palisades;

And how, behind them in a straight west line,
Scott's mountain lies,
The Lehigh River, Youngstown, Kankakee,
The Mississippi, the Muscatine,
And the boundless Plain,
And then Cheyenne,
And Salt Lake City, and Truckee;
Until at Sherwood or Fort Bragg
Moves the Pacific,
Frowned down upon by many a mountain crag.

The sky above the Palisades
Of old Hoboken strives to say
That there are cities, rocky grades,
Rivers and prairies of unrest
Far west,
Far away.

## GETTYSBURG

Amid the hush of the distant hills, which house
These sleeping meadows, oak leaves loosen and fall
Across the sunlight and along the rhythmical
Wash of the air upon this shore of boughs.

Leaves drift around the bronzes. But over the grass
Of the field where Pickett's men defied
The grape-shot and the cannon, and still died,
The shadows of October's clouds re-pass.

No shouts arise from the vanished garrisons.
No sound is here of wounded man or steed:
Meade stares at Lee, and Lee at Meade
Across a mile of pasture, eyed in bronze,

Where flies the solitary crow. Beyond
The spires of Gettysburg, the skies implore;
Nearby the cattle graze, and grackles soar
Where the air is tranced as by a wizard's wand.

This stillness is the indifference of the sky,
Of the tranquil Muses behind the mountains hid,
Who suffer Fate's beginning, nor forbid,
Nor ask the battle, nor mourn the tragedy.

Still they are brooding in their fanes afar,
And now they stir the oak leaves with their breath,
Saying there is no life, nor is there death,
Nor victors, nor defeated, nor fame, nor war;

But only music at last out of the dreams of these,
As the one reality which overtones the mime,
The landscape, nations, races—even Time,
Quiring eternal Nature whose heart is peace.

from
*Poems of People*

(1936)

# THOTHMES: CENTRAL PARK AND THE DRIVE

This is the shaft of syenite
Which Thothmes on the Nile
Raised to the sun god's smile
By the temple of Horus, the lord of light,
When Rome was not, nor Watling's Isle.
This is the self-magnificat
Of ibis, beetle, and lotus flower
By which Thothmes the theocrat
Eternalized his power
With hawk and priestly hat:
"Thothmes am I, beloved of Tum,
Who gives all life and majesty
In Egypt and in realms to be
For endless time to come."

    \*    \*    \*    \*    \*

The drift on Heliopolis
Was sifted by the Centuries,
Who played the sand game as they laughed
And tumbled Tum, but left the shaft,
The cryptic syenite.
For Tum fell down to dreamless night
When rose Augustus Caesar's craft,
And down the Nile and to the sea,
Where sailors saw the Pharos light,
This granite needle bore, and laughed
At Egypt's bended knee.
And cold Augustus spurned the hand
Of Cleopatra, doomed in war,
And made Barbarus governor
Of all the Pharaohs' land;
And, mocking Antony's opened vein
And Cleopatra scepter-stripped,
Set this needle up and chipped
Imperial Latin: "In the reign
Of Caesar, Barbarus did erect
This shaft to Caesar's Nile domain,
With Pontius architect."

      \*     \*     \*     \*     \*

So stood it, firm as adamant,
While Christian blood and Turk were spilt;
So waited it for Vanderbilt
In the ruling days of Grant,
When Thothmes' shaft borne on a bark
Was brought by Gorringe, U.S.N.
Across the outer sea, and then
Was placed in Central Park.

This is the parapet and dome,
The cruciform, the flaunt of flame
For one who bore Ulysses' name:
Captain of Shiloh, whom caprice
Of Fate raised to this wonder tomb.
"Let us have peace," he said. The same
Was carved: "Let us have peace."

      \*     \*     \*     \*     \*

This is the grave of a little child
Named by broken-hearted parents
"Amiable," near the tomb of Grant.
"Man born of woman..." you know the rest—
Carved too, with spirits suppliant.

This is the river on whose breast
The *Half Moon* sailed, which Hudson gave
His name to ere he passed from men
With no memorial grave.

This battleship, with those Marines,
Soon takes our governor newly made
To Christianize the Philippines.
Beyond is Jersey's palisade;
Beyond New Jersey is the West,
Where sinks the sun again.

# WEEK-END BY THE SEA

    I.

Far off, the sea is gray and still as the sky;
Great waves roar to the shore like conch shells water-groined.
With a flapping coat I step, brace back, as the wind drags by;
No ship as far as the seam where sea and sky are joined.

I am watched from the hotel, I think. *Who faces the cold?*
*Why does he walk alone? 'Tis a bitter day.*
But I trade dreams with the sea, for the sea is old
And knows the dreams of a heart whose dreams are gray.

Two apple trees, alone in the waste on a sandy ledge,
Grappled and woven together with sprouts in a blackened mesh—
They are dead almost at the roots, but nourish the sedge;
They are dead and at truce, like souls of outlived flesh.

I have startled a gull to flight. I thought him a wave:
The white of his wings seemed foam, breast hued like the sand-hued roll.
When a part of the sea takes wing, you would think that the grave
Of dead days might release to the heights a soul.

    II.

I slept as the day was ending, scarlet and gilt
Behind the Japan screen of shrubs and trees.
I awoke to the scabbard of night and the starry hilt
Of the sunken sun: to the old unease.
Sleeping, a void in my heart is awake;
Waking, there is the moon and the wind's moan.
I would I were as the sea that can break
Over rocks, indifferent and alone.

III.
I have climbed to the little burial plot of the lost
In wrecks at sea. West of me lies the town;
Below are the apple trees, pulling each other down.
Children are romping to school, ruddy from frost.

How the wind grieves around these weedy wisps,
Shaking them like a dog who sniffs from patch to patch.
I try the battered gate, lift up the latch,
And enter where the grass like a thistle lisps.

Lost at sea! Nothing thought out or planned!
What need? Thought enough in a moment that battles a wave;
What words tell more? And where is the hand to engrave
Words that would tell so much for the lost on land?

## THE RED CROSS NURSE

Aiken the artist, who was painting Sirens,
Used as a model Helen Vandegrift.
Starving amid the theater's environs
She posed for Aiken as a shift.
Naked atop some boxes (for the rocks),
Her blondined hair upon her bosom loosed,
She told him, as he painted, of the fox
Who wooed her, won her, left her so misused:
Left her to surgeons and a night of horror,
Grappling with death, attended by a nurse;
Left her, he said, to be his country's warrior—
Left her for duty, not his purse.

So Aiken, hearing, painted. Then he thought
Of the money prize for making a lithograph
For the war, where courage interwrought
With tenderness, and mothering on behalf
Of soldiers, would the heroic souls upheave
Of boys for war. Calling her then to dress,
He pinned a red cross to her sleeve
And painted her, down-gazing in gentleness
Upon a wounded soldier who looked up
In happiness, with eyes that strove to bless
Her white hand giving him the cooling cup.

So painted Aiken. And as snowflakes drift,
So over the land was scattered the angel face
Of the artist's model Helen Vandegrift
Until in every window it had a place
Of village shop, on every city wall
Round which the starved youths gathered, passion-stirred
For love and war, that they might bleed or fall
To be so loved and chosen by a word
From lips like hers.
               Meanwhile the rapid Marne,
And Château-Thierry where La Fontaine dreamed
His fables, waited for them who thither streamed,
Seeking her face. By many a peasant's barn,

In many a thicket where the bullet screamed
And faded out, or where the searchlights gleamed
Of airmen, over meadow and haunted tarn.

# THE GRANDSON

What's evil and what's good,
And how they may be weighed,
And where the balance lies,
What mind has understood?
There is the instance of the Perkinses,
And Captain Tanner, *viz*.:

First, it was wrong for Perkins to divorce
His wife—no doubt the answer's yes.
And why? It made unhappiness
For her true heart, of course.
By parity of reasoning, as they say,
'Twas wrong for Perkins' heart to stray
To Captain Tanner's daughter, Valeria—
No doubt of that! For otherwise, 'twould mean
There is no moral will, environment
Is all, and man is a machine
Worked by the stimulus of the Fates' event.
So much for Perkins' wife and for
Valeria and Perkins.
                        But there's more:
There's Captain Tanner. Did he have
A right to happiness, though you prove
That Perkins and Valeria should waive
Their hope, give up their guilty love?
For what should Perkins still have kept
His marriage vows intact,
If paid for as the Captain crept
With weariness which racked,
Going about his daily task
Wearing an idle, smiling mask
To hide life-emptiness,
World-loneliness?

But all such soul equations were re-formed
When Valeria married Perkins; when she bore
A son and named him Theodore.
Then Captain Tanner's soul was warmed;

Then sunshine on his life began to pour.
At morn and night, we heard the Captain saying
To Theodore, his grandson, cooing, playing,
"Up, little man, a soldier be!
Shoulder arms now, one two, three—
Fight as I did at San Juan:
Press forward, forward, forward, on!"

You never saw a heart so glad,
Such happiness the Captain had.
All life for him was changed, remade,
When what was once his solitude
To Perkins' first wife was conveyed:
The Captain's ecstasy ensued
By just this fateful trade.

Now for the grandson. Though we scorn
Perkins as a man forsworn,
How else had Theodore been born?
Suppose he means much to his kind
As statesman, thinker, or a mind!
If not, just leave out man and wife:
Did Theodore have the right to life?

from
*More People*

(1939)

## OLD GEORGIE KIRBY

Old Georgie Kirby, who for forty years has lain
Beneath the sky amid this boundless pasture,
    With rich blue grass for vesture—
His curses ended against the ruinous rain
Which drowned his bottom-land and spoiled his corn—
Was brought to nothingness as quiet
As the sky above, the fiat
Which made no answer to his blasphemous scorn.

For when the rain came and his corn was drowned,
He stood and shook his fist against high heaven
And mocked the violet levin,
Pitching his curses against the thunder's sound.

Defying God, he said "In ancient days
You drowned the world, so do it again, old devil,
And make these hollows level
With water to the hills! Blot out the ways
And roads to town, throw open windows and doors
In your revengeful sky, and wreck my labor,
And flash your lightning's sabre—
God damn it, I don't care now how it pours."

His pious neighbor, old Nathaniel Page,
Expected Georgie to be struck by lightning
For blasphemy so frightening.
But Georgie lived to eighty years of age;
He lived to bury wife and every child
And build this picket fence, here in this meadow
Around their graves, on which the shadows
Of hawk and crow float from that reviled sky.

Nathaniel Page himself has reached no peace
Greater than Georgie's in the silent prairie.
Here in this cemetery,
Though rain falls and deep thunder stirs the trees
And rumbles the hills, and shakes what bones remain
Of Georgie (cursing no more the lightning, thunder,

Or flooded fields), himself thereunder
Is a fellow worker now with storm and rain.

# NATHANIEL PAGE

Nathaniel Page loved God with soul dissolved
In gospel love. He thought his own transgression
    Brought flood and rust and Hessian
Flies on his crops, and so his heart resolved
A deeper penitence, a faith contrite
Before the Awful Power which ever brooded
Over the prairie, changeful-mooded
As thunder clouds or summer light.

A cyclone in the night, that passed around
The house of Georgie Kirby with no ravage,
    Smote Page's like a savage
And laid his barn and corn-cribs to the ground.
Old Georgie laughed and swore; Nathaniel prayed,
And searched his soul for evil,
    Believing that the devil
Was sent by God for heaven disobeyed.

Six miles of sky divide the several graves
Of these two men. Page's is in the village,
    Georgie's where the tillage
Still takes the flood, and where the winter raves,
And where the wind drives over the lonely plain.
Under six miles of sky, you ponder
    Their God-mood, as you wander
Down hills, by woodlands, and through Bowman's Lane.

## QUACK-GRASS

This land at first was overspread with clover,
Bluegrass and spears of timothy here and there.
Somewhere, somehow, another kind of grass
Got started, and John thinks the seed was blown
From fields about. I didn't know its name.
John called it quack-grass, since it simulates
The hue and form of useful kinds of grass,
But is unlike them, and has an enmity
For bluegrass and for timothy. When I knew
This quack-grass, it had taken all the field
And had all other grasses choked to death.

I looked into the matter, and I found
My land beneath the surface of the soil
Was just a mass of matted, tangled roots.
For quack-grass spreads by rhizomes, which send up
Their stems all seeded, and shoot into the earth
These multiplying roots, which underground
Creep everywhere in secret greediness
And hunger and contempt of other grass.

Then how to rid my land of such a growth?
I found it can't be done, hardly at all.
A remnant of a root will propagate it;
Fire will not end it, nor a deal of salt.
A plow can scarce be driven through that mass
Of roots that grip down two whole feet or more.
I started out to fight, and after years
Found still these rhizomes creeping underground,
The stems like foxtails waving everywhere.
What can you do when roots creep underground,
And when the mower merely clips the stems
And when the plow, though tearing up the roots,
Leaves pieces that take hold and fructify?

Well then, if God or Nature makes the choice
Of quack-grass to defeat all other grass,
And eat the soil up with a mass of roots

That take the earth— I say what is there to do
But rip those roots up now and then and make
Great piles of them for a fire, since you can't
Eradicate all of it from your field?

## LANDS END

This is the farthest West: the journey's dead-wall,
The sea at last, which stays all going forward.
This shore permits but pacing, back and forth,
By these sheer cliffs where perches the mateless eagle;
Where, far below, the eternal tides are dark.

There is no turning back to Springtime pastures,
Nor rambles in the hills, nor happy idling
In villages, nor rapture days in cities,
Nor fellowship with hands that reached this shore
In former days, and vanished into air.
Strength is still left, to face these walls of granite
And say the little that remains is little;
To accept the prison rocks that bar retracing
The meadow lands of summer winds and suns.
Here the sea drifts, and here there is a murmur
Of zephyrs in invisible sails, the whisper
Of waves that wash a hull concealed by mists.
But he who has marched hither, never shrinking,
And labored as a gleaner in harvest seasons,
May walk this shore with unaffrighted will.

Why see again a country that underfed
The heart's deep hunger, never quenched its longing?
Although this shore is not a destination,
Is not a haven but a bourne, a Lands End:
Making the visible sky and universe
Poor for the famished heart which ever grows
Larger with understanding and with longing
As life shrinks down, and narrows along the way
And leaves the soul, through losses, so much the greater.

But there's a gravity in the coercing sky
Which pulls the spirit, and breaks its pride and freedom,
And says "Surrender, cease the futile fight.
Find peace in union with the One, forsake
The Many of gleaming lures and false reports.
Come to Me, and no longer will I recede.

It is not the horizon that has diminished,
It is yourself grown shriveled, having starved.
No longer strive, resist, feed on yourself,
Be separate—but rest on me and live,
Not in estrangement, but by me sustained."

Year after year, imagination gathered
Into itself the roar of Time, the madness,
The tumult of humanity, the world of grief.
Now these must counterpoint the sea and listen,
As to a shell, to the burdens of stilled music,
And match them with the dirges of the deep.

Not wishing to return to a traveled country,
Unable to go farther, this coast must one
Pace back and forth, where there are muffled voices
Of waves that beat upon the stones below,
And sea winds whispering from the echoing grots,
Saying "Endure," saying "Endure, Endure."
Here one may sit, upon these granite benches,
And follow the restless gulls that wheel the sunsets
And trace the outlines of phantom islands afar;
Or watch a cricket on a spear of sea-grass,
Or mark the eagle on a spire of rock.
There on the heights he eyes the swimming sea
As lonely as the dead are, or this shore.

That world-ache of the long interior country
Is turned the petrifaction of this granite,
The pitiless Medusa which makes bloodless,
And heaps this shore with flesh transformed to stone.
That country's voice now mingles with the sea's,
And thus life's music lingers here by Lands End,
And thus the world of memory remains.
The years are here, as gulls above the waters;
The rocks are destiny, which at last supplant
All hands of friends or lovers along the journey.
They may be clasped, but never with responding,
Even as hands of flesh grow hard and cold.
They promise nothing, they are deaf to love.
Mute, they are now the ultimate withholding
Of justice which the world has ever denied.

These cliffs are breasts of Fate, being breasts of stone,
And still one's dreams and bring tranquility,
As ended breath brings peace. And they reveal
The mock of love that mocked hope on the way;
And they catch light above the sea's domain,
And gather rain cooled in the granite heights.
They give a sanctuary to the eagle,
And to the cricket, and to the heart's defeat
Pausing at Lands End, with no other luggage
Than a depth of thought that matches with the sea's.

Here I will pace this ledge above the vastness
Of restless tides, and etch with straining eyes
The phantom islands from their blurring hues.
And, guided by the creaking of the rudder,
Locate, perhaps, a sail that weathers storms;
And rid my breast of this constricting thought
Which comes from self-reliance, and has failed
To bring a peace. If peace there be, it must be
In union with a love whose gravity
Cannot be stayed, which crushes or has its way.
It must be by a yielding to the current
Which flows through all things, by swimming with its streams.

from
*Illinois Poems*

(1941)

## NEAR FOURTH BRIDGE

Here in the swamp where the dulled river sweeps
To the Illinois, the sand flats are aglow
With smartweed in the bottoms, there below
The hills on which the oaks are fast asleep.
It is November, but a butterfly
Stumbles along the air now growing harsh;
And, like a man in death, the marsh
Lies stiff in silence under a sunset sky.

A hawk sails overhead, braving the sun,
And crows flap flying toward the wood;
Night deepens, and absorbs the solitude.
A zephyr out of nowhere seems to run
Along the waste of cattails, and reveals
An inner meaning—as if the summer's face,
Or some memorial thing, sought now this place
Of noisy mallard ducks and blue-winged teals.

Out of the sky they circle to the shore
Of rattling stalks, where the cold willows stand,
Barren willows in a forested land.
With whirring wings and quacking, with a roar
Of wings, they blot the sun; the frozen scum
Around the cattails dims, the sunset's light
Grows faint because of their descending flight.
Silence creeps like a wave, for night is come.

Still down they fly, like autogyros that wheel
With level planes and vertically sink
Through dregs of sunset to the silver-steel
Gray of the waters, splotched at last with pink.
Down, down they drop, and make the waters splash,
And with rejoicing swim among the reeds.
And now the faraway horizon bleeds;
The sun is gone with one expiring flash.

The hunters have departed. In the East,
The planet Jupiter sails like a cresset borne
By magic and no hand. Mists make forlorn
The waters, rising as that exorcist,
The hooded night, convokes them. Behind the hill
The sun has hidden, and the marsh is caught
As by enchantment. Finding what they sought,
The ducks are silent and the marsh is still.

## HAVANA, ILLINOIS

Against the sky like a laundry rack,
The bridge of the river showed.
Red lanterns, where the draw was turned
In the midnight water, glowed:

They burned like a wolf's eyes down and up
The Illinois dark and lone,
To show the steamers where they could pass
Between the pillars of stone.

At midnight the tenders turned the draw,
And hung red lights at the edge.
There was no chain, no gate, no bar
To guard the open bridge.

And there at the edge of the bridge's floor,
A hundred feet below,
Was the river that eddied around the spiles,
And eddied to and fro.

At midnight Denny Cullinine
Came out of Harry Grier's,
And got his team and drove to Taylor's
For just a few more beers.

Then out of Taylor's he came at last,
And drove to the bridge unbarred.
There was no taker of tolls, no chain;
There was no one on guard.

The boards of the bridge floor rattled beneath
The trot of his horses' feet;
They trotted along to the open draw,
Then started to retreat.

They reared as they saw the open space;
They stumbled, about to trip.
But Denny cursed and urged them on;
He cursed and plied the whip.

He did not know that the bridge was drawn,
Or what was the horses' fear.
His courage was like a hungry wolf's
With those deep drinks of beer.

He stood up in his carriage then,
And gave them lash on lash;
They leaped and trembled, they cranked the wheels
On the bridge-rods with a crash.

He jerked the lines till the cruel bits
Tore at their lips and teeth;
He cursed and lashed them with the whip
Till they leaped to the stream beneath.

With one last struggle to save themselves,
They leaped as Denny saw
Why they had stopped and striven so
At the edge of the bridge's draw.

Down, down they pitched, in a tangled mass
Between the pillars of stone;
Down, down they went, and Denny had
Just time for a horror-groan.

A fisherman had heard the clatter
Of hoofs from the farther shore;
He heard the yell, and the water's splash,
And then he heard no more.

He rowed to the place where Denny fell,
But nothing was there to be found:
Nothing but eddies that came and went,
By the pillars round and round.

Next day they dragged the Illinois,
And dragged it here and there;
But neither Denny, horse, nor buggy
Was found, for all their care.

Three weeks later, they found a body
By the river's shore at Bath....
Some said that poverty wrought this evil;
Some said 'twas heaven's wrath.

Some said that Denny had killed a man,
And lived for months in fear.
Some said he had lost his farm,
And therefore had taken to beer.

## WILD GEESE

In the still midnight along the Houghton Road
My uncle Wilbur Masters and I so often walked,
Hearing on high the sudden honk
Of geese, where heaven overflowed
With starlight before the moon had sunk.
October scents were drifting from the fields, the hedge,
The oak woods and the withered sedge,
And hollow stillness cupped the sleeping scene.
Above, there was that living wedge
Of breasts, of wings, of bills
Streaming toward the Mason County Hills.

They dodged between the stars by night bestrewn;
They sailed across the moon
As swift as ghosts. Far north, above the rimmed
Dark hills, like sparks from a forest fire
Sparkled the stars, which lured them as they skimmed
Through light and mists, fulfilling their desire
For olden haunts, for seeds, protected nests,
Obeying the urge of life that never rests—
Even as Uncle Wilbur and I
Along the country road
In darkness walked, with wondering breasts,
To the old farm house on Sandridge,
The loved abode.

from
*Along the Illinois*

(1942)

# THE PRAIRIE: SANDRIDGE

To contemplate the prairies is
To fathom time, to guess at infinite space,
To find the Earth-spirit in a dreaming mood.

In Illinois the prairies are a soul,
A muse of distance eyeing the solitude.
It is not the mountain's soul, the lonely face
Of the desert, nor that of the many-hued abyss
Of the canyon, though here there is no goal
For the eye but grass, and levels to the horizon's rim.
They are a sea of earth, and they have waves
When the winds sweep over them and dim
And brighten the fields, and the shadow of the hawk.
The cloud is hurried over miles of grass,
Dotted with barns and houses, long-heaped graves
In country yards. Breaking the stillness, a cock
May crow afar and charm the sleeping air,
As white clouds with an ancient mission pass.
Crows may fly over, as the sunlight's glare
Mingles with stillness which the grasshopper
Scarcely disturbs with his somnolent whirr.
But to the north, a river's flow is shored
By the drift of hills enclosing prairie land,
And over all a blinding light is poured
In which the banners of the corn expand
And breathe and flutter, gathering a hoard
Of sweetness for the harvest.
                    Above all
Is the spirit of the scene, the mystical
Presence: not wholly nature, and not man,
But made of these: made even of the dead
Whose living hands reaped here, and who began
With prairie-plows to subdue and cultivate
This vastness; and who met the human fate
And sank into this earth. They interfuse,
With Deity added, these voiceless miles
Of meadows; they have become the earth.
Kincaid, McDoel, Ensley, Watkins, Miles,

Houghton, and Masters speak here as the Muse
Of this domain. They whisper of toil, of mirth
In the gracious days before the Republic—grown
With the lust of trade to power imperial,
And battleships to man the farthest seas—
Sapped all this realm, and gnawed to the very bone
The substance of their descendants, to the fall
Of liberty and bread; even as tyrannies
Did this, for now is tyranny
Masked as a benefactor. A slow disease,
Progressive, fatal, has ruined liberty.

No lesson can be learned! The ancient wars,
Corruptions, thefts, degenerating the mind,
Give no instruction now; none, saving this:
Man cannot ruin the good earth. All the scars
Of spears upon Acadia, Macedon,
Thessaly, Sparta, did not blind
The recreative shining of the sun,
Nor take away the soil's fertility.
These prairies will be here after man has done
His worst to ruin life. As long as the sea
Rolls round the earth, these prairies here,
Surviving the death of hope, of liberty,
Will brood upon the centuries year by year
And tell of plenty, peace, domestic joy,
And labor recompensed, and rugged health,
And hearths un-anxious, and honest wealth
In this beneficent land of Illinois.

## INVULNERABLE EARTH

Attila, Genghis Khan, Napoleon, stormed the earth
And towns were wrecked, fields razed, countless men were killed.
Yet Earth remained uninjured, and life renewed its worth:
Towns arose on ruins, fields again were tilled.
Feeble men that crawl this sphere are as silly ants
Digging habitations, killing mates for food.
Earth is still invulnerable: smiling when troops advance,
Unmoved when bombs are rained, wasting guiltless blood.

Those who fall glide into earth and are earth again.
They become invulnerable, deaf and blind as she.
Let the siege guns thunder! What's a diving plane
To the rocks, to the wheat fields, to the scathless sea?
Look at Shiloh's shambles, walk the Wilderness—
Where's the wound on Selnac Hill, where at Waterloo?
Earth resumed her peace again, deep and passionless,
And men became triumphant, being earth anew.

What was blood at Gettysburg to the resting bones
Of those who died at Yorktown? what to Washington?
The hero of the Hermitage lies still as valley stones,
Unmoved as even earth is to battles lost or won.
For earth cannot be wounded, and men find healing sleep
With her, as a mother folding them in blissful rest.
She smiles indifference on them when they, dying, weep
In fear of the sealing spell of her soothing breast.

The dignity of mountain heights once more is theirs;
Their freedom is a pine tree looking to the stars.
They are a river flowing so swiftly that it hears
No lumbering of legions, no thunder from the wars.
And none can wake up Jefferson, and none disturb the dreams
Of Shelley, Poe, or Wordsworth; of Lincoln, or of Lee.
Invulnerable as earth is, though the syren screams,
They are as safe as granite is, as free as hills are free.

## PRAIRIE WIND

O prairie wind! O ever-seeking soul
That wanders like time and, even when at rest,
Surrounded by silence, speaks the unfathomed whole
Of human feeling by your kindred breast:
You voice us, for we as souls are wind
Who wander, seek, lament, are blind.
Sole audible genius of eternity,
Intangible being hastening ever between
The orphaned earth and homeless infinity,
Mourning for what man is, what earth has been,
And for his aching heart, his hopeless woe—
O unseen presence, singing the ebb and flow
Of human sorrow, O winged and free
Spirit over the meadows from slopes below
The Mason County Hills, who touch the strings
Of hearts, and make them question what you are
In all your wanderings
From magic lands, some place afar;
In moments rare, our inner eye perceives
Unutterable things half understood,
As when you spring from whispering leaves,
Parting the branches of a wayside wood,
And breathe upon the heart a secret bliss,
A fleeting something of an inwardness.

How you companion the clouds! The fleeing shades
Of clouds upon the meadows! How you race
The thistle wings of mists up distant hills,
Which vanish at the top where sunlight fades
With the sun obscured! But soon into their place
Swift shadows like eagles sail, as the prairie stills
Or mounts to billows when the sunlight dims,
Or brightens to blues where the high hawk swims.
O miracle of bright March days,
When windows whine and there are witchcraft-shrills
Around the house's corner, while woodland ways
Protest your breath with many a creak
As the dead limbs of the sycamore

Sway in the valley where you roar,
And rushes whisper, and apple trees
Break the enchantment of light and speak,
Then lapse again to meditating peace.

Like a deserted soul across the plain
You moan, as if you sought but never found;
You cry with longing and with patient pain,
Unable still to hide a cureless wound.
The killdeer and the meadow lark are borne
Aloft, astray from their intended flight;
The plowman's coat is flapped, by winter worn,
And the manes of horses tousled by your spite:
As when, with thumping hoofs and nostrils wide,
They end the furrow by the side
Of leafless poplars stretching to the light.

For now the rolling land is growing warm;
The snow has melted, and the winter's storm
Has fled before your voice. The April moon
Slits the evening sky, and the planet of Spring
Burns in the West where the prairie dims.
You will speed over the plowed lands soon;
Your breath will flutter the thrush's wing,
And bring the rain until the rivulet brims.
You will bear the scent of fragrant smoke
Where the farmer is burning brush,
Or scent of blossoms where wild lilies choke
The banks of streams now growing lush.

Spring passes, and the summer. All tossing grass,
At last the banners of the corn grow mute
And in the orchard where you pass
Your presence is made known by falling fruit,
As apples thump the blasted sod
And grapes grow purple, and the wild-pea's pod
Shakes for you at the thistle's parachute.
Again the windows whine, the corners groan;
Out of dream distances you come
From beyond the horizon, where one star alone
Twinkles above the prairie as partridge drum;
And crows are calling, and the evening hearth

Gathers the family for comfort against the cold
Which enters the fields and byways of the earth,
The first cold-cider air
Of autumn, when sheep turn to the fold.
And now across the plain you fare,
And sway the walnut and the maple boughs
Around the old farm house
Until the moon is as a sphere of gold
Tossed up and down,
Or along their ragged branches is rolled,
As out of the river valley you roar and boom,
Or flutter the splendor of the sinking sun
Beyond a lamp's light in a prairie home.

Again, at last, out from the North you blow
The blizzard filled with frost.
You hurtle across the fields the falling snow
Until the summer paths are lost.
The fireplace roars, the chimneys whine,
As if some creature stood without:
Complaining, asking like souls that pine,
Like souls that long and doubt.
And we who hear your howling all around
The smoke-house, the wood-house, and the walks
Of withered honeysuckle and hollyhock,
And far afield, with wonder dread
Draw close and listen to your sound,
Or look from windows at the driven cloud,
The whipped weeds, the tree tops tossed and bowed.

O prairie wind! O voice of the infinite,
Coming from storm clouds and from skies sun-lit;
Dawn-traveler, valley-seeker, visitant
Of ruined cabins, stricken fields, lone graves
And pasture pools, and of the green extent
Of growing corn, which in autumn no more waves
Banners of satin, grown with frosting scant—
I would know what you are, and what you say,
Crooning at windows, singing as you stray
Long miles from the hills, moaning in coigns
Of house walls, shrieking as you cross
The rippled rivers. Is it death or loss,

Is it life defeated, is it hope that joins
A consummation never, that you sing?
Are you eternal light given voice, a wing?
Are you infinity, pacing the never-ceasing flow
Of human feeling, and with soul too vast
For man's weak heart? O unquiet soul,
Touching man's thought and waking desperate dreams
Through earth-sounds or the evening's glow,
Or wrecks of clouds that sail the blast,
Or the moon you toss and roll
Or float upon the current of prairie streams:
Are you a lamentation? an endless dirge
For dying man? for lone lands where his bones
Waste else unsung, while earth's defeated urge
Is chanted by your mourning tones
That seem to speak all tragedies, all wars,
And the bright indifference of far visible stars?

## SPRING LAKE VILLAGE

As in an old print, dreamy and dim, remote—
Across the lake, fixed in the summer air
Where no sound is, afar but near,
Spring Lake the village stands, or seems to float
Above the shore of sail and motor boat.
The village spire, human and yet eternal,
Pierces the sky, evoking what is expressed
Never, so deep it slumbers in the breast,
Where strives the infinite with the diurnal.

Along the road, crossing the little bay
By the sun-parched graveyard, beneath
The shade of maples lining the country way,
The village comes to view; then disappears
At the turn of the corner, where the breath
Of Lake Michigan comes over the rhythmic reeds.
Here houses hide, and here the piers
Are lost; and here the church's spire recedes
Below the sky-line, and the river gleams
Now here, now there, along a wide expanse
Of rushes, motionless as in a trance;
While nearer-viewed they bend and dance,
And whisper summer dreams.

The sky above is blue, is infinite,
With white clouds thick as dolphins swimming
The Mediterranean streams. The lake is lit,
Then darkles with the dimming
Of the sun cloud-hidden. Now entering
The village, all the wonder of distance fades:
Here is the concrete walk, the wooden spire
Of the church; here youths and maids,
Workmen, shopkeepers, whistle, talk and sing.
But down the street the shore-line comes to view,
And one can hear the boats bump, see the sails
Unfurled and flapping, and see beyond the hill
Where grapes are grown above the grassy swales
Which shore the water, where the sad curlew

Wades, and where gulls flap in the landward gales.

Around the lake and out of sight
Of the village, there is a hill that slopes
To the water's edge, and on that hill a house
Between pine trees, haunted by hopes
That passed, of swift delight
That winged with robins among the apple boughs....

from
*The Harmony of Deeper Music*

(1976)

# VOICE OF THE VALLEY

The leaves whisper finalities.
The grass gestures, asking "What is loss?"
The clouds sum mortalities;
The mountains look afar, over the Atlantic deep.
They say a poet is asleep
At Skyros.

The mountains say "Shed no tear,
Grieve not for what has been,
For what has never been,
For what will never be.
You should be as the sea,
Without pain, without fear."

The green valley under the evening sun
Says "Let the wild world run."
The mountain says "I have been here forever,
I shall forever be here
With clouds and the flowing river—
Shed no tear."

## THE SLEEPERS

Between the unawakened souls and those who sleep,
This Earth is for the living who dream and weep,
Who war and labor, droop with weariness;
Who win, who lose, who waste the day, who reap.

So much I think of the millions on millions who
Once walked this Earth, and then as soon withdrew;
I think of the many millions to be born,
Who will emerge from silence to this view.

To sleep forever after life—to wake
For brief years haunted by the heart's deep ache—
What is it for? And what can be the Power
That creates, only to waste its work and break?

Why this strange world, given us for a space
So little (and given as it were a grace),
Then taken away, and with repeated life
Given to others emerging for the race?

Is it then strange that man with madness burns,
And life itself no final wisdom earns?
No: for the mind but mirrors the scheme that wakes
The sleeper who to sleep so soon returns.

## AT MIDNIGHT IN MYTILENE

The moon is gone, the Pleiads have set,
Midnight is over the hills.
Atthis has departed with Andromeda;
I lie alone.
I know not what to do. I am in two minds.
Life is always thought that does not solve the heart;
Time like a dark river flows forever.

Though the muses have brought me the true prosperity,
They have led me with pain into many scenes,
Into many hearts.
I have entered the wars, the Olympics,
The hearts of lovers walking by seashores under the moon,
And those driven by Fate to the Leucadian Rock.
I see white-sailed ships on blue water,
And hills of grapes where there is song.
Earth's beauty consumes me;
The lyre makes my heart leap like a faun,
Then sink as a faun struck by an arrow.
For the passion of women is in the lyre—
O the agony for understanding the passion of women!
Love makes a poet of the veriest boor;
What has it not done to me?
It has made me a slave with Psyche
Under the cruel eye of Aphrodite:
Through her I have lost everything but immortality.
Through her I have found desire that never ends,
And rapture that is brief, is frail.

Where now are Telesippa and Megara,
With whom I lived pure and beautiful hours,
Lost with them in music
And in verse?
To be so lost is to mingle heart with heart,
Thought with thought; that is the delight of music and verse.
Where are Anactoria, Gongyla, and Euneica,
Who listened to my instruction in verse?
O, that you were with me tonight, Gongyla, my rosebud,

With your Lydian lyre!
Desire in my heart forever hovers about you;
The very sight of your robe always thrilled me.
You never bruised me as did the faithless Phaon,
Smitten with dullness, thinking always of himself.
There is little peace, little beauty, in love for a man.
Once again would I mingle
The music of words with the harmony
Of your face, your breast,
And interpret each by the other,
As the sun and the sea exchange enchantment.
There is a cloud gathering in the east, north of Egypt.
Death is in the world now,
But that cloud will bring fear and shame into the world.

Neither a navy of ships
Nor a host of soldiers are fairest of things—
The beloved one is the fairest of all.
I love delicacy, and the beautiful;
These are the passions of the honorable,
Of the virtuous.
For this love I have become a reproach
In Lesbos and the Isles;
I am of ill repute therefore with the people.
What if my face is engraved on the coins of Mytilene?
What if the melodious Alcaeus praises my verse?
I am but hyacinth trampled by the shepherds,
Which, though crushed, still blooms purple on the ground.

I loathe the courtesans of Naucratis,
And in chief that Rhodopis.
What vileness for my brother Charaxus
To marry Rhodopis, that black and baleful bitch!
Sorrow and longing divide my mind.
Nor does it help me that such women as Rhodopis
Will lie unremembered, and will have no part
In the roses of Pieria,
Which belong to me and Atthis.
May my brother be rid of Rhodopis
And choose a mate in Lesbos
With breasts sweet as violets.

For the theft of Prometheus,
The gods sent plagues of fevers and death,
And the passion of women on earth.
For the theft of that fire
Men were punished with the fire of women:
More mysterious than any flame,
Seeking always a kindred flame.
Evil it is that that flame
Consumes what it lives by,
Or cannot set it afire.
Men are straw, or green wood:
They take fire but do not make a light.

Only Alcaeus and the poets know what love is,
And even they do not understand as I understand.
The gods have made men inadequate to women,
So that they do not see each other aright.
Only with Atthis and my beloved women,
When my girlhood was all flowers,
Have I found beauty and happiness;
Never for long, even with Phaon.

I am small and dark and ill-favored.
I am a star entangled in a marsh.
I am like the nightingale
Whose ill-shapen wings enfold a little body.
But I have a name which fills the world,
Even as the song of the nightingale
Overflows the woods of Lesbos.

Would that my paps could still give suck,
That my womb were able to bear children!
Then I would come to another marriage bed.
But age marks me with a thousand wrinkles,
And love comes not to me
With his gift of happiness and pain.
Gone are those hours with Atthis and Anactoria.
I lie alone, thinking how every woman desires,
How every woman is denied
Sleep in the bosom of a tender comrade.
When beauty hurts and no more heals,

Then Hesperus, who brings the child home to its mother,
Should lead the lover to the Leucadian Cliff.

## MEDUSA

This is the face, with its penetrating eyes,
Merciless and all-knowing, that in time
Gaze on the helpless flesh of men, surprise
Spirits that love, that labor, and that climb
Over steep rocks, turning their breasts to clay,
To stone, in the swift sculpture of defeat.

I saw a cinema of dead cells: they lay
Like lava pellets, or bubbles on the moon,
Like cobblestones in a Pompeian street.
All life had left them. They were ghastly gray;
They were as shattered glass by mischief strewn:
Medusa had gazed on them.
                              Whence was fled
The spirit that made them whirl, dive, divide?
Being now lifeless matter, being dead,
Was there no motion in them to provide
Motion in turn? They seemed beneath
The moon's sway; they seemed luminous particles
Of the moon that has no water, and no breath.
The moon, it may be (where Medusa dwells,
Presiding over tides and lives as death)
Moves life at will, but is by life not moved.
Then is there, in these cells
So Gorgonized, a something not all bereft
Of motion, but still active, though unproved?

Perhaps with this regard one hope is left:
As substance still the nucleus goes on
Dancing, though slower, to the harmony
Of deeper music, that of trancéd stone.
With cells of flesh, therefore, this thing may be.

But why should I be made to guess the stage
Of being after Medusa stares the flesh?
Why mine the pain that nothing can assuage?
Why mine dishonor and a barbéd mesh?
Why turned to me forever but one side

Of the sphere, and that a hope; while like the moon
The other side is never by men descried,
Which may be eternal darkness, or a swoon
Of ice where souls, like lifeless cells, are brought
By winged Medusa?
                    But this much I know:
Medusa, like a ghost
Rising all suddenly where she may choose,
Transfixes men to their soul's innermost
Being, and fills full with granite juice
Veins, nerves, and heart; eyes, hands, and lips.
What happens then to flesh made syenite?
Medusa knows, perhaps. Like a snake that slips
Into a crevice after its deadly bite,
She steals away, her witchcraft being done—
Death is Medusa, and turns men to stone.

## THERE IS LABOR WHITHER THOU GOEST

No heart for any soul is much distressed:
Work must be done, food eaten, time employed.
Meantime, the core of dead cells has no void;
For matter even as matter there is no rest.

In that sense you will never be at peace.
Then if, in death, cell-energy have thought,
When you to the darkness of the grave are brought
Your life will go on, will not cease.

Why pity you, when your flesh has become
A part of other whirling? There are two fights:
One for earth tenants under heaven's lights,
One for the darkness of the resolving tomb.

There are for spirits, as for flesh, enzymes
Which change, transform by a katalysis;
Whose working is of earth's creative bliss,
Though without apprehension, without dreams.

Shelley described this as the sea of love
Into which we sink: a sea unconscious, deep.
But as in life our flesh works while we sleep,
Death may an endless labor prove.

# IN MEMORY OF ALEXANDER DEXTER MASTERS

No heart's sin is more punished than the sin
Of that forgetting of a heart which dies.
Beauty and Truth with wide, accusing eyes
Will smite a recreant memory for what has been.

What though the noisy days, the stress of life,
Cover the dead? What though the power of thought
Less vividly can summon what is not?
Hours come that bear the knife:

The silence and the uncomplaining lot
Of the dead wound like a sudden strain
Of music, and fill the heart with pain
For loveliness forgot.

In that hot summer fifty years ago
You passed in agony, and I have wandered on
This intervening time, forgetting you were gone
For days, for years—how did I so?

You were a boy miraculous of face,
And you were gifted with ethereal mind.
How strange the Fate that to your heart assigned
Five years of life—and then your vacant place!

And then our tears; the grave; then back to the house
Resuming life. And then the passing days,
The years, and change; and living, which betrays
For its poor self our wondering brows.

And the long years in which no answers come
To us, who ask why you were born to die
So soon—where you departed to, and why
The tomb remains the tomb.

*from* VIGNETTES FROM VERMONT

    II. *Charley the Hermit*
Them dogs won't bite; they keep the foxes away
From my chickens. How do you like my house?
I built it of old pieces that I picked up.
Look inside if you want to. That kitchen stove was give me,
And that old cot where I sleep came from the Masons up the mountain.
Purty disorderly, ain't it? Cans, bottles, old clothes, everything—
That gun there was in the Revolution in New Hampshire.
I killed a fox with it last winter.
Yes, it was purty cold, and snowed in;
I had to send my cow up to the Masons' barn.
Sit in this chair in front, if you want to.
I washed that today, that piece of green cloth;
That's purty, ain't it? Found that in the woods.
Looks like a sash or somethin'.
There was a lady's handkerchief there, too;
I've got that in a drawer in the house.
No, I never hain't married. I came from Massachusetts,
But I've lived in Connecticut and everywhere.
Been here twenty years. I picked this place;
It's so purty, and by a nice brook just over there.
It has trout. I'm all right here. Don't mind livin' alone,
But don't like thunderstorms. When they come up,
I walk up the woods to the main road
And sit on old Mrs. Comstock's porch.
I did that this mornin' about three o'clock when we had that storm.
Old Mrs. Comstock came to the door in her nightgown.
She knows my ways. I make a good livin'
Selling bouquets, and baskets which I weave.
Look at my flowers and potatoes!
I'm happy here, all except the thunder and lightnin'.

### III. *Old Mrs. Comstock*

I'm breakin' up here. Had an auction yesterday;
Sold everything in the house but my Bible and rockin' chair.
Brought just a few dollars. Why, my maple bureau
Sold for a dollar and eighty-five cents!
My cookstove was about to sell for a dollar,
But I gave the auctioneer a wink:
I'm goin' to give it to Ruby Deems, a blind man
Up the road about a mile.
I had to get into town. Too lonely here. I'm seventy-seven,
Been livin' here forty years; hate to leave.
This is a good house. Fine sugar lot back there,
Never been touched. A nice mowin' piece, too.
Can't stand another winter here. Last winter
Snow was piled four feet up around the trees,
And didn't see a face for weeks. No mail.
What was worse: Tom, my brother, had just died.
It was awful lonesome on that account.
We had lived here together since my husband died.
I hain't got no relatives now but a sister;
She's comin' today to help me into town.
My husband died five years ago. Son died before him.
I used to weigh a hundred and sixty;
Now I'm down to a hundred and eighteen.
It's the loneliness, and grievin' about my brother.
I'm just cookin' a piece of bacon with some string beans.
Maybe I can eat a bite, but a body can't eat good
Eatin' alone.
There's a few books on the floor there you can have
At your own price. My husband used to read
That Samantha Allen book to me, and laugh.
That *Tributes to Mother*—I don't remember where that came from.
I've had it forty years.
Excuse me a minute, I must look at my beans.

### IV. *Ruby Deems*

I live just down this dirt road about a mile.
I can tell light by this here left eye;
The other is out—had a cataract. They cut it off.
Eye got infected. My wife and oldest daughter
Are workin' at a summer hotel;
The other seven children are with me at the house.
Folks thought I was goin' to be a girl,
So they named me Ruby before I was born
And stuck to it when I came a boy.
I have a fine garden this summer:
Look at this here fine potato; I dug it with my fingers.
Goin' to show it to Charley Powers up the road.
That's where I'm goin', about a mile.
I don't like to walk into town:
Them trucks turn corners too sudden.
On a country road I'm all right.
Can't manage small seeds. When they grow up
I can't tell 'em from weeds when I weed.
Oh yes, I help with the hayin'. I'm an old man, forty-nine.
All summer get tired just weedin',
Or any little thing. Have to go in the house and sit.
Yes, I smoke cigarettes—used to chew,
Used to chew twenty cents' worth of plug a day.
Quit and took to fine-cut. Quit that and began to chew gum.
Came back to a pipe; hurt my tongue.
Guess I'll go on and see Charley Powers.
Goin' to saw wood for him this fall.
Good day!

# PLANTING TREES AT TOR HOUSE

Jeffers planted two trees: one for George Sterling, one for me,
There near Tor House with Lobos Point in view.
Jeffers smoked a pipe while the earth was spaded.
He smiled, he chuckled at times, and the Pacific
Came to the shore like the shadow of a great cloud
And slushed half audibly, like the wind around a cliff.
Sometimes there was a roar as a rock repelled the water.

George Sterling stood there, his cheeks streaked with weariness,
His eyes dim—not with dreams, but with unhappy reality—
And Jeffers smoked and sometimes spoke.
Sometimes he chuckled. As always with me,
I was the witness: I took it all in,
Seeing the weariness of Sterling, and Jeffers' youth,
His strength, his repose like a young eagle's
Who nests in the mastery of a mountain.

Then, after the trees were planted, George Sterling and I
Took a walk on Lobos Point, where old cypresses
Stretched their tortured branches. Years of strong wind
Had stretched them to point to the mystery of the sea.
They were mesmerized explorers who had landed,
Who had suffered enchantment, and become fixed in the rocks.

Fifteen years have passed since those trees were planted.
Within a few months of that day, George Sterling's body went through
    fire
And his ashes filled a tin cup. The weary eyes,
The streaked cheeks, became flakes, the stuff of powder.
I am still a witness, thinking today about those trees;
Thinking of Jeffers, whose voice rides the mountain wind;
Who is both Tiresias and Amphion,
With eyes piercing through the land, the cities,
With music that moves rocks and lifts them into walls.

## NOT TO SEE SANDRIDGE AGAIN

Amid these city walls, I often think
Of Sandridge and its billowed land between
The woods and hills: where clover, red and pink,
And corn fields, oat fields, wheat fields, gold and green,
Lie under skies of speeding clouds serene,
Where gardens know the robin, the bobolink.

The yellow road that travels by the hedge,
The rail fence, till it slants the gradual rise
Of farms toward the upland fields that edge
The Sangamon, touched by descending skies—
All this I see; this is that loved Sandridge,
All changed, but changeless in my memories.

Orchards and strips of timber, walls of log,
Barns, windmills, creeks, even the Shipley Pond,
Have vanished like the early-morning fog
That hung above the swales, and far beyond
The pastures, where the patient shepherd dog
Followed the farmer, beautiful and fond.

Earth even may change, but if the love it stirs
Remains, is Earth then changed? If man must pass,
And generations of cattle; if harvesters
Themselves are gathered, and old men sink like grass
Into the quiet of the universe,
Yet memory keeps them, they are never less.

That is eternal life for them, for me.
For what is living, save it be that what
Was beauty is preserved in memory?
If gazing on a dead face is to blot
What the dead was in life, so not to see
Sandridge again may be the better lot.

# THE HILLS OF BIG CREEK

You hills around Big Creek, you fields of corn
Whose glistening banners flutter the summer sun,
Behold me once again! After long years
Of wandering in the world, and after cities
East, west, and south explored; and after lives
Laid on my being one by one, like these
Layers of rock which over this little stream
Show the earth's age, each stratum flooring down
And stealing from itself the era gone,
Do I come here once more: and see how earth
Retains its aspect while the race of men,
Like the new creatures of each passing spring,
Are born, grow old, and mix with earth again.
The future to which I looked when, as a boy,
I gathered flowers here, or these valleys walked,
Or raced these hills, has come and is the past.
Time, like the water flowing through these banks,
Takes on the images of fleeting things:
Clouds, sunlight, stars, the spring or winter sun.
That which has flowed will flow. And future days
Were Time, as even the days before were Time;
While what was mirrored in the creek was life,
Was grief or happiness, or love, or loss,
Which vanished ere the water moving on
Changed the essential mirror.
                            Scarce a face
Of those I knew about these hills remains,
Their beauty to revisit, and recall
With me, if memory served us, what we felt
Or dreamed or suffered forty years ago.
All, like the generations of the birds
Which made these woodlands ring about us, even
Their nestlings of the after-years, are gone;
While the same song is sung, and while this stream,
As it were the very water that I saw,
Reflects the cloud shaped as it was of old.
Cattle are here, and once again the corn
Rises to make the boundless acres green,

Remembering not the fields which men long dead
Planted and gathered. And here again are youths
And maidens who repeat my happiness,
My wonder at the sailing cloud, my shouts
To comrades hidden in the fastnesses.
They know me not; know not that, as a boy,
These hills were mine which now are theirs. O Earth,
Growth is forgetfulness, and within ourselves
Life has its eras, and with senseless stone
Walls in the heart, till to its inner core
Remembrance, like a fallen acorn caught
Between the crevices of great boulders, dies
For light and rain, grows pale and withers too,
Forgetting what it was.
                      And those my chums,
Who my delight companioned, after years
Of world's affairs, of failure, of success,
Of marriage, children, all that we call life,
Have glided to the grave. The future days
To which they lifted eyes, and sang the heart
Of hope and longing, came to them and fled.
Time flowed between their helpless fingers, who
Were but the mocking cloud upon the stream.

If death end all remembrance, what is life
Which blots remembrance of the soul you were
But death? What am I, even, who only know
That this branch, called "I," back to the parent trunk
Of parent days extends—but cannot relive—
Their feelings, visions, thoughts? This latest twig
Of being, tipped with present life concerned
With just this day, lives not the life between.
It has its leaves, which have no memory
Of the many leaves along the branch's growth,
Or what they felt of rain and summer sun,
Of cold and frost.
                  Nor is my being saved
From the death of living to this oblivious tip
By the mind's summoned image of a face,
A girl's, who in obliterate springs with me
Looked on these hills. Nor is that death annulled
By love, confessed out of the conscious mind

Which graved what was. To know, the heart must feel;
To remember, it must live again its love.
Hence is this death not overcome by thought,
Acknowledging the grief of sundered hands
These thirty years gone by. All this I know,
But with the mind: as if an eye should bud
Upon the branch's tip, and backward look
To the parent trunk; yet being but an eye,
Without a heart to make the vision live,
Should stare without a tear. And not to feel
Is not to live; it is the loss which life
Exacts for living; it is the death which creeps
With years into the flesh.
                    She has become
One with these hills, which I but look upon
With an eye for nature still, yet deeply changed.
She is to me as if she never was,
Or ever was, a part of earth. I see
This landscape in a light that shows each bare,
Each empty spot, each shrunken height, each vale
Made narrow, and these grassy banks reduced
By the cold glare which is Eternity's.
That we forget the soul we were is death;
But that we neither live the past nor grieve
Proves Death the healer, since he heals in life.

## A NEW DAY DAWNS

When the sprinkled stars begin to dim,
And the hills emerge from shadows;
When the last bat drifts to the woodland
And the wrecked moon sinks in the west;
When the corn stands still like a man in thought
Looking ahead at something, ready to speak;
And cool air stirs from the hollows
And carries the sweet of clover meadows,
And the cattle lying in the warmth of the dust
By the old rail fence breathe deep—
Then soon a rim of light spreads round
The rim of the hills: the sun is rising,
A new day is at hand!

I have loved this land America.
I have loved it from coast to coast
With a love that aches, that has no words.
The desert, the apple valleys, the shores of the Pacific,
And those of the Atlantic and the Gulf
Have seen my steps. And I have climbed the Rockies,
And traveled the roads of the mesa country,
And the wheat fields of Kansas, and the breadth of Texas;
I have wandered by the rocky brooks of New Hampshire,
And over the hills of Connecticut.
I have paused by old churches, mills, and mansions,
And read ancient headstones.
A new day dawns—
Farewell, sweet land!

Already there are signs of change.
The bats are hurrying to the shadows,
The corn and the wheat sigh prophecies of the full light;
The dip of the landscape toward the uplands
Gradually reveals the houses built by hands
Already forgotten, where fields are now tended
By grandsons of a fresh breed,

Who race past the new schoolhouse,
Nor remember the old—
Farewell, sweet land!

The sun has set upon our generation.
We have lived through the night of war and change
To this hour when the morning winds
Waft the smell of clover blossoms,
And the mystical stirs of the dawn
Announce a day not ours but yours, you young,
To do with as you can.
I have given you my best, America,
Out of a love that hurt my breast.
I may have misused the time;
I never wasted it—
Farewell, sweet land!

There will be many nights of stars, and dawns of wrecked moons,
And bright easts calling to labor.
And you, generation after generation, must keep and enrich the life
Of these coasts, these valleys, these fields.
To you I leave it—
Farewell, sweet land!

*Uncollected and Unpublished Poems*
(appearing for the first time in book form)

# SPOON RIVER REVISITED

Ed, I've been down to Spoon River.
I've seen the town,
I've seen the people,
And I know the town and the people,
And I am scared.
For they say down there:
"A little leaven leavens the whole lump,
Wait and see—
Spoon River will be Americee!"

They took me all around in a Ford.
They showed me the town and the country.
And I saw all the churches and newspaper offices,
And the banks, and the court house,
And the jail.
And the stores and the canning factory,
And the wagon works.
And I talked with the judge and the ministers,
The lawyers, teachers, and politicians.
And everyone said:
"A little leaven leavens the whole lump,
Wait and see—
Spoon River will be Americee!"

And they drove me all around in a Ford—
'Twas Editor Whedon's son who drove me,
And there at the edge of the town, we passed
A field all grown with weeds.
And the son of Editor Whedon said:
"That's the racing track we closed.
There was gambling there, and a clerk in Rhodes's drug store
Embezzled some money to play the races.
And that gave us the lift we looked for,
And so we closed it."

And as we drove around the square,
The son of editor Whedon said:
"That feed store there, where you see those boxes
Of hog remedy in the window,
Is where old Burchard had his saloon.
We closed the saloons here;
There will never be saloons here any more.
And over that store across the street
Is where Johnny Taylor had his room
Where the boys played poker years ago.
We don't allow that anymore.
There will be no poker rooms anymore."

And then he took me to the circulating library
And introduced me to the librarian,
A woman with creaking joints and nose glasses.
And she told me they didn't allow no books there
Written by bad men,
For only a good tree produces good fruit.
And she thought Byron and the French fellows
Were bad.
And that anarchists and disturbers,
And people dissatisfied with the world as God made it,
Should be suppressed, as they were suppressed
In the library of Spoon River.
And she twisted her face and grinned until her glasses
Got askew on her nose,
And her false teeth half fell out.
And she said with a laugh: "'a little leaven
Leavens the whole lump', we say here.
Wait and see—
Spoon River will be Americee."

And then this son of Editor Whedon
Showed me a gymnasium they had closed,
Because they had some boxing there.
And he said: "Brutality and violence
And things that make for disorder
Are not allowed in this town."

And this was next to the canning works.
And he said: "They had a strike there once,
But the Circuit Judge enjoined the strikers,
And broke the strike.
And now there's no discrimination
Between non-union and union workers.
But the union fellows left,
And now it's a non-union place
And an open shop.
For we don't allow no sedition here,
And no harangues on the street,
And no meetings in halls
Where the purpose is to disturb the world
As God made it for us here.
We have our churches,
And our lectures,
And a good movie theatre
Where pure things are allowed
That any girl of sixteen can see.
And since you ask what the people do
To fill in the time:
The men work; they are thrifty, sober, God-fearing;
They save their money and stay at home.
And the women keep house and read out of the public library.
And the young people are taught right and wrong,
And get married when they are of age."
So I said to the son of Editor Whedon:
"Who's responsible for this ideal community?"
(At the same time kicking my own back with my own foot).
"My father is," he said with a smile.
"And I'm driving now to the cemetery
To show you his grave.
Would you like to see it?"

Says I: "I'd rather see that grave
Than the pyramids of Cheops."
And over it was a stone with a little cupola, like,
Enclosed with window glass,
Making a kind of cabinet.
And in the cabinet
Was a tin-type of Editor Whedon
Taken by Penniwit the artist.
And as I stood there, I said to myself:
"Wait and see—
Spoon River will be Americee."

(*The New Republic*, 23 November 1918)

# I AM AMERICA

The song of America, mighty in battle: behold,
I am the world's great hope made manifest in the flesh.
Look at the men of my loins, confident, powerful, bold;
Dreamers of dreams that are new as the spring is fresh.
Look on my daughters who walk where the winds are sweet,
Losing the trammels of time, seeking the newer truth.
I am America, passionate, keen and fleet.
The nations of old have their use, but I am Youth!

Remembering and repaying, I come at the cry of France;
Cherishing England's glory, I stand by England's side.
I barter, travel, adventure, live to the full romance,
Heeding the while the words of the voices that prophesied:
Washington, wise, patrician; Jefferson, lover of men;
Lincoln the maker of harps from the salvage of guns,
Giving his heart-strings for strings for the song to rise again.
Look at my daughters, the muses, the gods, my men.

The secret stir of my spirit mixes the blood of the races.
I shall have none for my own but my breed and clan.
I take the spirits of Babel, the stranger faces,
And make them into my image: American.
None shall inherit my portion who sulks or resists,
Hides under cover of seeming an alien desire;
Tyrants, oppressors—and the spawn of them, royalists—
Brawlers, disturbers, must melt in my forge's fire.

Millions of soldiers for peace, and countless treasure
Out of my great abundance, harking the voice of the Age:
A new day dawns, poured from Eternity's measure.
Freedom shall be the rule of the world and its heritage.
Wherever the sun springs forth, it shall gladden the free,
Yellow and black and brown born into a wonder world,
Kept for the living of life by hands instructed of me.
The flag of crossbones and skull shall forever be furled.

I am America, hands prest close to my breast;
Looking across the waters, patient, subduing my grief.
Come back, O Sons, when the battle is won and the pest
Of the wild hog's madness dies for the world's relief.
Out of the spirits treasured in words that are hidden,
Bring forth to use, remembered, lay close to heart.
Build and cease not; out of them you are bidden
To the moulding of domes, lest the glory of me depart.

Bring for my use the wisdom of Europe, my mother,
Forgotten or never possest, to be made my own.
Whatever is profitable bring me: tho' it come from another,
I will make it flesh of my flesh, and bone of my bone.
Come back, O Sons, not hardened alone in war,
But rich in the visions of progress, garnered up for my hand.
I am the evangel America, blest with a rising star.
You may turn or delay me, but I at last shall command.

(*The Independent,* 23 November 1918)

## CLARENCE DARROW

This is a man with an old face, always old.
For even when he battled and hated, in light
Of an irradiate urge against the world,
And the wrongs and follies and idiot things
Of the world made his step quick and his look
Fierce and swift, he looked old even then.

There was pathos, too, in his face and in his eyes,
And early weariness; and sometimes tears in his eyes,
Which he let slip unconsciously on his cheek
Or brushed away with an unconcerned hand.
There were tears for human suffering, or for a glance
Into the vast futility of life,
Which he had seen from the first, being old
When he was born.
      He was always a poet too,
And a poet is the barometer of the world,
And a vicarious sufferer for all sufferers.
He was a poet who found clay for his modeling
In those who were martyred for striving
For the weak, the despoiled; the Prometheans
Who tried to carry candles or lamps for the world
And found their light snuffed by Envy or Greed
And themselves left in darkness, bleeding.
He did not seek the role of Promethean himself,
Because of the whimsical side of him, the penetration
Which saw through crucifixions to the joke behind
The hill of the crosses: the world of hunger and sex,
Banquets and latrines, the whole unending serial
Of animal function draping itself in immortality
And calling itself humanity. Nevertheless,
He grieved for the Prometheans more
Then he grieved for the poor. For he saw
That the poor are dull, and hence are poor;
That the poor are faithless and untrue,
As much as any; and that their desire is
For the things which the rich have; and justice
Means that to them, or something like it. Yes,

He grieved more for the Prometheans, the sacrificers,
The dreamers, the diers for causes; grieved
And laughed, because of their belief
In progress, or perhaps millenniums. Then as time
Went on, he smiled for them; and yet
With all other faith swept away, and belief in something
Must be to keep the viability of life,
This feeling for the Prometheans remained.

One time I spoke of God to this man,
And he looked quick out of an open window
Then back at me, and I know what he thought—
I caught it. He thought if there was a Force, a Mind,
Which suffered the mind of man to evolve,
And tortured it all the way, and tortured it
More and more as it became keener to see,
And keener to feel, then he wished for strength
To resist this God, and tell him to the last
That He was wrong to make the world so, and man
To torture so.
          Well, if he believed in a God,
He also believed this God had willed the world
As evil and life as evil, and pain in excess
Of happiness or peace. And his sustenance
Was in believing this, and finding confirmation
About the truth of this.
          In all my days I have found
No sadder man, gladder in his sadness.
I have found no man who went his way
With less excuse or reason fashioned for himself
Of going at all; and no man
Who believed more in truth and good will,
Though he backed them only with their own
Self-evident need for being.

  This is Darrow,
Inadequately scrawled, with his young old heart,
And his drawl, and his infinite paradox,
And his sadness, and kindness,
And his artist sense that drove him to shape his life
To something harmonious, even against the schemes of God.

 Sept. 27, 1922

  (*The New Republic*, 27 May 1957)

# THE RETURN

### I.

When he returned he saw the porch at first,
Where cornices and pillars showed decay.
The entrance door was scaling, seemed accursed.
The water troughs had rusted quite away,
And it was raining, and the house was cold;
And over the wires for lights and telephone
A vine hung, thick as moss; and the rain tolled
The minutes in a minor monotone.
He stood beside a window and looked out
Into a yard of tangled grass and leaves.
And the rain swished from a half-broken spout,
And gusts of wind blew water from the eaves.
When she came in she was singing, and asked him then:
"Are you not happy to be home again?"

### II.

He turned and saw how yellow was her face,
Creased where the collops met along her cheeks;
And saw her greasy jacket with torn lace,
And the drab hair that crossed her brow in streaks . . .
Then looked again at the autumnal morgue
Of long-neglected bushes. Then away
His fancy hurried to the Luxembourg,
And Chopin's valses he had heard that day
A month ago. Then too there was the rain,
But lyric rain that mingled with nocturnes,
And no pain then, save as delight is pain;
And not the ache of clouds or broken urns.
She still was standing in the door, and said:
"If you are ill, you'd better go to bed."

### III.

He made no answer, still looking at the yard,
Then from his pocket took his handkerchief
And, as he drew it out, let fall a card,
And flung some powdered petals and a leaf.
The scent thereof revived that afternoon
Of Chopin and a walk, a slender hand
That held his arm and kept his heart in tune . . . .
Now why did she continue there to stand,
And note first moments of the prison cell?
He knew she could not guess what he had lost;
She was too dull, and too invincible.
In a few seconds, then, the room she crossed,
Picked up the card, and said: "The dinner's late,
Calm down and warm yourself before the grate."

### IV.

And to these words his heart gave out a fume
Like livid coals where water has been thrown.
And that was all the hatred that his doom
Aroused in him, to this exhaustion grown.
His hatred had been raging fire along
The years of separation; now at last
He could feel nothing but a callous wrong,
Except this yard and room that held him fast.
He stood beside the window without thought,
But for the thought the trees had, and the rain.
He knew he hated her, but hatred wrought
No passion to reply, not even pain.
She spoke again: "Be cheerful and be good."
Then she went out and left him where he stood.

### V.

He sees her as the face of age and death,
And fights her hands, which draw him into dust:
The envy that would cool his passion's breath,
The disbelief that mocks his love as lust.
Thus envious and world-sustained, she hangs
About his strength and drags him like a growth.
And if he sinks, should there be any pangs?
He still can swim, and why not swim for both?
And as for love not ever hers nor lost,
And in her faded life no more to be,
Then hate for everyone shall be the cost:
If she must be unhappy, so shall he.
The world, if it believed in love, would shun
The ruin of three souls instead of none!

### VI.

He must return, or have the one he loved
Headlined and pictured in the daily press,
Her hatred was that naked and ungloved.
And he returned to save that sordidness.
But once at breakfast, as it came to pass,
He did not speak because his soul was ill,
And then she choked him with the poison gas
That he'd returned to her of his own will.
Blinded with fury then, he rose and slapped
Her face, and slapped her cowering at the wall.
He would have throttled her, but something snapped
In him. He saw that murder might befall,
Then turned and staggered out of doors—but where?
The world was all too small for such despair.

### VII.

He lies in darkness like a tranced cocoon
Awaiting wings, and dreams of life ahead.
The door creaks and she enters, pauses, soon
Flings back the coverlet and gets in bed.
Now shall he strangle her? For there's the scent
Of banal powder on her; he compares
Roses and lips, and midnight passion blent
With whispers, to these desiccate despairs.
Now shall he strangle her? She yawns and twists
Her lolling flesh; he summons strength to speak—
"You must not stay here" —doubles up his fists—
But instantly she turns the other cheek
And whispers, "Well, good night. Tomorrow, dear,
And daily, you'll be better, being here."

### VIII.

When he comes down to breakfast she awaits,
And says, "good morning, dear;" begins to serve.
Her aura is a spider-gray. The Fates
Are not more gray, and were he moved to swerve
From his disdain by her phosphorent smile,
The ashes of her face and eyes restrain
A yielding to her meekness, which is guile.
He sees her as America: the chain,
The rusted iron, the insipid mass
Of deathless protoplasm, which increases by
The scalpel, satire. She begins to pass
The toast, and talk his soul into a lie
Before the public, with an outward show:
"The concert is tonight; I wish you'd go."

### IX.

A robin woke him at the break of dawn
And pursed his heart valves like a purse with strings,
And wounded him for springtimes that were gone,
And for uncaptured joys of vanished springs.
And what was spring? And what were springs to come,
Since springs all golden through his hands had slipped?
And, like a worm with early frost grown numb,
He turned upon his pillow, terror-lipped.
But deepest agony of soul was this:
His ruined spring quired by the song they heard
There near the Luxembourg, when their waking kiss
Caught between lips the rapture of the bird.
Below him in the kitchen was her tread,
Between the stove and sink with feet of lead!

### X.

He has slept heavily, awakened tired.
He feels so old and weary, numb and dull.
The restless flame of interest which fired
His soul, the search for beauty, both are null.
Amoeba-like, she has enwrapped his soul;
And sucked the ichor of his soul, whereof
He sprayed creation with an aureole.
He hates her; she denies him other love.
She has stripped him of other love but hers,
And severed hands that touched and knew his hand—
And, now she sees him tangled, ministers
With a kindness viscid and a cunning bland.
He rises to depart. She says "Tonight
Come home; it gives the children such delight."

### XI.

He sees he is a dead man walking still:
For life is love, a friend, a relative,
And all of these are vanished. Were he ill,
Or starving in a park-seat, none would give.
There was a time (but then he had no need—
O sorry jest!) hundreds had made amends.
Now hundreds ignorant of his past would read,
And say, "Has he no relatives nor friends?"
And so he's dead for having lost the hands
Who knew him, or lived current with his fame.
But life is life when fruitful in commands,
And life is death when one is but a name.
Yet he has her, and she says: "Why not see
A movie at the New Academy?"

### XII.

Love is a voice of music; hate is dumb.
Love is unfolding; hate is a turning-in.
Hate is withdrawal till the flesh become
A numbness to which nothing is akin.
Love is a growth which every day puts forth
New blossoms out of life; hate shrivels up
The flesh and drives the blood in like the north.
Love fills, but hate turns down, the empty cup.
Love stretches hands of flesh; hate tightens fingers,
Shrinks and retreats, grows brief and thin of breath.
Hate hides and broods; love shows itself and lingers.
Love is a name for life, and hate for death.
All ignorant of this, she says: "O please
Be happy, be contented, be at ease."

XIII.
He has outlived, almost, the stuff which life
Stored up for living. Wherewith shall he live?
And what would be to him mistress or wife,
Since forms are shades or shapes diminutive?
He stands upon a mountain, looking down;
He stands without, and peers the window through.
The country, city, village, and the town
Are playthings only, neither false nor true.
He is beyond life, yet not given to death.
He sees with eyes that look from other spheres.
He wonders if he keeps this mortal breath,
Since he has neither laughter, no, nor tears.
He wonders if this be the price he pays
For wisdom and for living many days.

XIV.
He rises at the morn, looks in the yard,
And tries with thought to build a better day.
He thinks about the world of men ill-starred,
And why should he be happier than they?
There are good men in prison; some are ill,
And some have walked the midnight without bread.
And some lie tangled in a broken will;
And if death be dishonor, some are dead.
Some, like Walt Whitman, rise to sit and wait
Another day through. What is God above
That this old earth is magnetized with hate,
And sleeps not, rests not, for the urge of love?
Thus thinking of his brothers, agonized,
His pain is lessened, being democratized.

(sonnets I-VI and VIII-XIV published in *Poetry*, September 1923; the original sonnet VII was deleted by editor Eunice Tietjens and is reproduced in Russell, *ELM* 196-197. The entire sequence as originally written is published here for the first time.)

# HYMN TO THE UNKNOWN GOD

O Thou, who art not Thou, Thou mind impersonal:
Thou light, whom as I hymn I praise as well
All beings and all worlds;
Nor do I lift Thee over heaven, nor stars,
Nor earth, nor men, the multiples of Thee;
Thou beauty not apart
From leaves of grass, from smallest things that crawl,
Mountains and seas and rivers. Utterless Thought,
Immanent in all things, whose broken rays
Are thoughts becoming stars; Thou who art all!
Thou infinite beauty, eternally the same,
Thou one reality beneath what only seems,
Perpetual motion and perpetual rest!
Thou pantheism of the poet's dreams,
And animism of the savage breast!
Thou life in earth, in insect, stick, and stone,
Thou mind transformed and made dependable
By thought that finds the law! Thou something known
To lovers of the invisible! Thou viewless flame
Eclipsed to our mortality! Thou darkness edged
With rainbow hues! Thou force insentient
In rock or sperm, that lifts itself to mind,
Works itself to spirit by sure ascent!
Thou source of eyes while being blind!
Thou Nature, cruel and indifferent,
Becoming conscience! Thou evil and Thou good,
Not merciful, unfaithful to man's hope,
But true to the living truth as source of life.
Thou the necessity of the atom's law,
And the imperative of man's moral code,
And giving it significance! Thou Unknown God,
Not to be feared nor held in awe
By men who are a part of Thee, as stems
Are part of the parent vine; and who with hymns
Become aware of that same living blood
And soul of the worlds. Let never heaven's vault
Be as a skull colossal, enclosing with crumbling weight

Man's mortal skull as an alien sphere at fault.
Thou art that heaven with its love and hate.

We listen, but cannot hear Thee;
We grasp, but cannot hold Thee;
We look, and cannot see Thee;
Thou appearing as existence,
Thou fading as non-existence.
Thou Light that flies, too fleet,
Thou formless, Thou defeat,
Thou failure which art persistence,
Thou germ of vast profusion,
Thou cause of our illusion,
Who see division where there is none,
Blind to the truth that there is One;
While good and evil, part and whole,
Are phantoms, mere appearance
Of the scene made separate by Time and Space,
The latticed windows of man's senses,
Robbed of the soul's coherence
While Thou art all, the film continuous.
All substance, impermanences,
Thou river ever-flowing
With waters luminous,
And ever art coming, going,
And art one stream forever,
And the same stream never,
Of which no one can say
It is not, or it is.

Thou whom at the solstice
Of winter great Confucius
Dreamed by heaven's marble stairs;
Thou whom Lao-tze found
By drawing in the snares
Of the senses of sight and sound
Until eternity
Was in himself, made free
Of all the world external,
And Thou the great eternal
Wert in him; and time was lost,
And Thou wert consciousness

Where time and space and form
Vanished to nothingness;
Thou in whom Buddha, in the forest,
Saw the true self as part
Of the eternal that restorest
The human heart,
And the life of man as karma,
The universe as law;
Thou whom Ikhnaton perceived,
As he built Amarna,
In the sun, the lily marshes,
And amid the great green sea,
And in the silence of his heart which grieved
For delight in Thee.

Thou whom rapt Cleanthes hymned;
Thou whom ancient India knew
As the sun's light, the taste in water,
Heat in fire, and as the wisdom
In the wise,
As the light in lover's eyes,
By their passion dimmed.
Thou whom Zoroaster saw
As Creator, giving light,
Lord of life and law.
Thou the dream of Leonardo;
Thou the meditation
Of the starry spirit Plato
With melodious inspiration.
Thou beloved of rapt Rabia,
Seeing sleep as meditation,
Kisses as the mystic union
Of the human and divine,
Love of Thee like wine:
Both the source of ecstasy,
Both intoxication,
Laying hands upon creation
And eternity.

Holy Thou art, but vicious,
Just, cruel, and capricious;
Loving and true, but faithless,

And leaving no error scathless;
Omnipotent, but without favor,
Omniscient, but no savior,
Unchangeable, but weak as light or water,
Compassionate, consenting yet to slaughter,
Long-suffering, but swift to retribution,
Consuming fire as jealousy, but glorious;
Making Thy way by evolution,
By pain, destruction, paths laborious.
Merciful but unmerciful, and all-seeing
To sharpen fangs; blind to man's higher being
Yet lighting the sun for grass and grain,
And giving life, and sending fruitful rain.
Author of peace and discord,
Winging the dove and sharpening the sword;
King, despot, gracious lord,
A rock, a piercing shard,
A fortress, but a dungeon, a jail.
Shepherd, yet conspiring with the wolf,
A father who lets his children wail,
A counselor guiding spirits to the gulf,
A guide who fools the blind,
A providence who denies,
Friend to Thyself and Thine, the wise,
Not heart, but mind!

Thou soul of the Andes and Mount Everest,
Fathomless canyons, the depths of the sea,
The vale of Chamouni,
Spirit of great rivers, and desert wastes,
And mourning shores:
There man can feel Thee, there find rest
As his heart adores.

Thou that art Nature,
Thou through whom the spiral clusters
Turn to stars, at last as dying stars
Are strewn abroad—
Thou unknown God!

(*The University Review*, Summer 1937)

## END OF AUGUST

Through the glass of the transparent afternoon,
The apples of the orchard and the leaves
Look as if seen through lenses of crystal stone,
And sphere with vacancy the wheeling scene,
Enchanted by sunlight. But when the breeze
Sounds his salpinx, and the semibreves
Of wind first dim, then brighten, the lowering gold
Of the westering sun which floods the empyrean,
Then all the orchard trees
And maples roar, and the upturned leaves are pale
As ghosts from the Erebus of delicate maids:
Unwedded youths who left the cistern shades
For life, as these for Summer start to wail
Amid the sound of crickets manifold
Which chirp from hill to dale.

The forested hills are billows of verdant floss,
Which bluer grow like thickening smoke.
But the nearer trees are brighter green,
Like fountain-freshened moss
Struck by the level splendor of the sun;
And these stand imaged and serene,
While by the stone wall rank burdock,
Late yarrow, goldenrod,
And buttercups with grasses overrun,
Dream with the devil vine, and lean
To hear the wild bean shake its rattling pod.

There is no sound save trees that roar,
No sound but of a shell
From some long, lonely shore.
There is no sound but crickets in the grass,
No sound but one's heartbeat, one's thought.
A presence is here, behind this spell,
Which should emerge and break the magic glass
And speak this mystery fraught
With watching eyes, which say
They look from a place aware

Of our desire, when we divine
The secret hidden in unsubstantial air
And almost see it, almost touch it: standing
Behind thin walls of sunlight crystalline.

(*American Mercury*, September 1937)

# LI PO

Li Po the Banished Angel,
So many centuries now lying on
The Terrace of Night,
Sees no more the moon above the city of Chang-an,
Nor the fair region of Yo-Yang
Where lived his friend Tung Tsao-chiu.
He sees no more the Yo Mei Mountains,
Nor the Min Mountains, far west of the Road to Shu.
Nor does he drink wine by the Yangtze River,
Nor in Nanking, nor Shanghai:
He is long a name, like the name of a mountain.
Mountains do not grieve that war shall never end.

He has become a height, on which
The beacon fires of his songs burn and go not out,
Showing wanderers the way to the good life
Of hospitality and song.

With the mountains, he does not remember
When the empire was wrecked, when the imperial army
Was slaughtered by the barbarian foe
And the bones of the slain were piled in the hills;
When beautiful buildings, porcelain, jade,
Were destroyed, were stolen,
And the poetry of an innocent people failed to soften
The hearts of conquerors.

Li Po lived sixty years,
Seeing his people in fear of the hordes
North of the Great Wall,
Seeing war and ruin and famine.
For more than a thousand years
He has been at one with the indifference
Of the East Mountain, or the waters of Tung Ting Lake.
It is more than a thousand years
Since Po Chu-i visited the grave of Li Po
By the river Tsai-shih,
There amid the pathos of endless grass,

Under a blue sky patched with white clouds.

These never die, never cease to be:
Mountains, rivers, and clouds from the sea.
And songs never die:
They are as mists around the slopes of hills,
As clouds on the peaks, tinged by the sun,
Through which armies march in vain.

(*Asia and the Americas*, March 1938)

## AMPHIMIXIS

Everywhere in creation is the urge
To enter in another, fuse, and merge.
Roots turn toward the earth; the church's wall
Attracts the vine; the electric current draws
Steel filings and arranges them by laws
In patterns star-rayed, geometrical.
There is response to touch, to earth, to light.
The chromosomes of cells detect the might
Hidden in heaven, in earth, and arrange their poles
Centered in fibrous stars: so flesh and souls.

Creatures at first bi-sexed—sponges and snails,
Volvox and flatworms—long for severance
That life may be increased, that heads and tails
Of the sperm may grow, the ovum's waiting trance.
But being severed then, they seek and long
For union; they divine that they must win
Oneness again, and by that fate begin
A life more individual and strong.
The genius of creation which made them two,
And divided their hermaphroditic state,
Drives them together then and makes them mate,
That greater life, more perfect, may ensue.
Think you of That! Call it the Secret Power,
Or call it God—which, hour by endless hour,
Stirs plasm and awakens it; which conceived
Sex as the way for life to be retrieved
From floating jelly! Think of That which made
The sperm and ovum, severally incomplete,
Then formed that great perfection, by the aid
Of fusion through desire that scorns defeat.
Oneness, autogamy, would divide, be free
For selfhood, then for union by ecstasy.
Oneness is loneliness at first, and then
A solace, a consummation for plants and men.
Whether it be in lifting from the mist,
From water, by a passion none resist,
Or whether it be—at last, the cycle done—

A sinking to the source and entering in
The ocean, where all living things begin,
Life's passion would be two, and then be one.

The hyphae of black mold on common bread
Are intertwined; the cells of ulothrix
Swim round until the ovum feels the head
Of the sperm, and then their substance starts to mix.
Marine life listens to the summoning sea
Which calls them by a wedding symphony.
So from the alga swarm the restless sperm
Seeking the egg; and so the rockweed's eggs
Are hunted by its male gametes which worm
An entrance, then their life no longer lags.
As malarial cells, which touch and conjugate
Themselves, shaped like a swastika, and then
Find heads and tails, so is it too with men:
Emitting life, love-driven, to penetrate
The waiting ovum, and enter and be lost
In whirling change for life exchanged and crossed.

For with an entrance made begins the toil
Of larger being: the plasm starts to boil,
To froth with destiny and secret dreams.
Granules are threaded; there are stars, spiremes,
And radiate lines, and spindles which in turn
Enter the spireme; union further thus
Wins an achievement, is victorious.
For union, oneness, do these creatures yearn.
Then there are splitting, halving, stars and poles,
As even later there are in our souls.
On higher levels, everything repeats
The self-same story: union, and life more deep,
Flowers till the consummation finds defeat.
The cycle being run, then there is sleep;
Or energies so fine the microscope
With their invisible movements scarce can cope.

Man grown to fullest stature, in mind complete,
Is nothing but a world-enclosed gamete.
Shelley and Shakespeare, larger than the swarm
Of human gametes, and of clearer form,

Prove that a man from microscopic life
Arises to a level where he feels
The frothing, the boiling, the surging strife
Which stirred in him when he was coils and reels.
And so he swarms, and swims, and dives, and darts,
And seeks to enter mysteries and hearts
Along the way of finding the high ovule
By which he may a greater being rule.
Is it heaven, is it God, that he would find
And enter in, and first if used and blind,
And then devoured, then by that union stirred
Gather more life? The truth is, everything—
Whether it be amoeba or man—is spurred
To seek more life, whatever be the sting,
The tragedy of transition. That's the Word
Which was at the beginning, and never rests,
In plants and animals and human breasts.

    June 28, 1938

        (first published in Ronald Primeau's article "Shelley and
        Edgar Lee Masters' 'Amphimixis,'" *The Old Northwest*,
        June 1975)

## HYMN TO THE UNIVERSES

I begin to sing now, not to the awful goddess Demeter,
Lady of glorious fruits and flowers and grain;
Nor to Pan, the over-ruler of Nature;
Nor to Earth, the Mother of all;
Nor even to the sun nor his divinity, Delian Apollo.
Lastly, I do not sing to Uranus, called heaven, the husband of Earth,
Herself once called the most ancient of created things—
But I will sing the infinite skies,
The Milky Way, wherein move the sun and earth
And the planets.
And I will sing star-clusters and vast islands of light.
I will rise above this whiff of air,
These puddles of seas and warts of mountains,
And sing of the vacuum which is the universes,
And of the thrilling darknesses,
And of the sky-rocketing nebulae
Which pulsate and recede from earth
Fast following the speed of light.

I will journey to, but not pause at, the Magellanic Clouds
Which are only eleven light-years from earth;
I will not loiter by the Andromeda Cluster
One million light-years away;
Nor at Pegasus, twenty-three million light-years afar;
Nor at Cancer, thirty-six million light-years.
I will pass by, after speeding one hundred and five million light-years,
The Leo Cluster; and go on, beyond Gemini,
Not tired with its distance
Of one hundred and thirty-five million light-years.

I will not stop in any of the five hundred trillion universes
Glowing with red, green, yellow, blue, and violet light,
All receding, all eternally expanding,
All changing into matter and back into radiation.
Beside these, earth is not ancient—
Earth is only eighteen hundred million years of age
While its universe, not to speak of the universes,
Is three billion years old.

I will go further into endless seas of space,
Where there is darkness and no breath,
Past star-clusters two hundred thousand light-years away;
Lighted by the self-sustaining light of mind
And thereby made kindred to the sun.
I will traverse the darkness of the universes,
Seeing that there is no end to space and energy,
And that man can conquer these wonders
With numbers and far-wandering thought.

Having so journeyed, I will return to earth
And consider liberty, the state, despotism,
Sin and salvation from sin, theologies and religions,
Poverty and incurable disease, madness and spiritual torture,
War, crime, irrational epochs, and the possibility
Of the existence of mischievous supermundane creatures
Who take delight in deceiving and tripping men.

I will think of love and what it is,
And why there are golden ages, and ages of crime and ignorance;
And why man composes music and verse;
And how madness strikes races and eras;
And why there are hostile breeds;
And why there are life logics, strong as mathematics,
Which advance, retard, destroy and deceive;
And why there are hunger and envy, strife and blood-shed;
And why idiocies flourish and are bequeathed;
And why man never finds an ultimate reason
For striving, for trying to be better;
And why the mind is irrational, and what thought is,
And why illusion abounds everywhere,
And myths lead and tangle human steps forever;
And why earth is too good for men,
Who make hunger in the midst of plenty,
Who kill and rob.

I will consider why nature exalts and debases,
And creates the loneliness of seashores,
And evokes the breathless ecstasy of mountain peaks;
And what it is that makes the human heart desolate;
And whether it is the suction of the receding universes

That pulls at his breast and draws his wonder on,
That fills him with ever-unquiet dreams.
I will declare that God is not a father
Who pities his children,
But is alternating darkness and flame
In infinite space, in infinite time.
Though life and earth are not enough for man,
Who is greater than either, I will ask
Why fear tracks his steps without ceasing,
Why death overtakes him, disregarding what he is;
And how he never knows why he began, or whence he came,
Or why he dies, or where he goes.

I will consider why his spirit is stirred
By the Mind that rules the universes,
But to no end save pain and loneliness:
No end that he can comprehend or imagine.

Howbeit, I will sing the spirit of man
Which, whether it emerged from earth and rocks
Or was separately created, is the transcendent miracle,
And may fitly face the universes as an equal,
And eye them with satire,
Wisdom, and solemn music.

(*The University Review*, Winter 1938)

# ON SEEING *TANNHÄUSER*

If flesh be sinful and accursed,
Why did the Word become the flesh?
Why was the soul sent in the mesh
Of blood and passion's endless thirst?

If flesh be vile, and thus doomed
To death, the grave, and sure decay,
Why heaven's promise, though entombed,
To raise it on the judgment day?

    February 24 1939


    (previously unpublished)

# THE TRIUMPH OF EARTH

Let down as by a rope into this cistern of twilight,
The flesh feels centipedes and hell-benders
About feet slipping in slime, while the eyes look up
Through the door of the cistern into the beauty of the blue sky,
And white clouds, and by night at stars and planets
And the miraculous moon: always these, whatever the cistern's darkness.
The ears hear music in the heavens from the spheres,
Which the shriek of rats and the slithering of serpents
Fitfully annul, until at times it seems
There is no music, nothing but the sound of crawling life—
But all the while there is music for attuned ears.

Here Janus rules, guardian deity of gates
(Which look both ways),
Gates reached by paths of ashes, hiding coals of fire.
Here right and wrong are shuffled together in the fury of days.
There is everywhere enough liberty for arguing both for and against,
For taking either side: all is matter, all is mind.
Here the mortal and the eternal strive,
And imagination struggles with reason.
Here it is only certain that there is nothing certain,
And every medal has its reverse side,
And false things are so like the true that no man
Can trust himself along these rocks: there may be a precipice.
Here it is good to know the country gods, Pan and Sylvanus,
For by the roadside are the insanities of shrines and crucifixes.

Here, if the soul had a mate, darkness and doubt
Might be better endured, and earth's absurdity quieted.
But men and women are not made to harmonize;
Their physical beings give them hostile minds.
Here man for an instant finds through woman the eternal,
And loses it in an instant.
As for our fellows, we are told by a man-god
To love one another, but the Supreme God made us
So that we cannot love one another;
We are formed of flesh and spirit incapable of loving one another.
We are parasites spawned and endowed with savage hunger,

And live in the cistern only by way of the cannibal.
Even imagination, which can heal, can lift,
Has an equal capacity to wound, to destroy;
And is used in age after age over the earth to wound, to destroy;
And by its envenomed divination knows the sensitive spots for stings.
Forgive your enemies, but also in the words of the prophet
Curse into hell all who resist the offered salvation.
Put them with misguided Judas, who was never forgiven,
Not even by him who counseled forgiveness seventy times seven—
This from the man-god, who has attained world-wide authority.
For there is only one path, even though human minds are lenses
Of differing strengths and adjustments; so that the wise,
So that the just, see one thing
And the fool, the bigot, the tyrant, and the devourer
See another thing; so that the daily record of events
Publishes one truth, and history with a longer perspective another truth,
And man at his peril tries to see aright—
What shall we do? For this is the triumph of earth!

Nothing in the earth is gauged ideally to man.
While his spirit is a part of earth's restless froth and whirl,
His spirit is also a spermatozoon
Seeking some ovum, it knows not which, for merging and growth;
Longing for God, yet not knowing whether God
Is the creation of the heart's desire or is a divined reality;
Not knowing whether it be better to doubt everything
Or to believe in something passionately, though deceived at last;
While everywhere there are traps and hooks
Baited with images of love and truth
In a world not enough for the human spirit, yet too much;
While the heart aches for something more,
And aches because the earth defrauds and deceives,
And aches because the will must be ever asserted,
Day by day, asserted or surrendered, and that is death;
And aches because the property and wisdom of earth
Must contend with the noise of quarreling superstitions
In this earth life, which envelops man in darkness
But keeps urging him toward the light:
This earth life which makes man dependent upon earth,
But rouses him to struggle for heaven
Through the dark side of earth, through the light side of earth.
We cannot prove whether life be good or evil—

That is earth's triumph. What shall we do?

Life after many years does not destroy hope,
Does not disprove the infinite, does not disprove a Supreme Mind
Working in the outer world, and in man's soul as well;
While man's soul, like the sea, is calm, is turbulent,
Is good, is evil, is beautiful, is vile;
Is full of uncomprehended currents, struggling between keen perceptions
Which see the surface and conceive hate;
Which see deeper influence by love and good will;
And so discovers man's heart and the world as good,
As dark or serene, as the day is foul or fair—
What shall we do?

The soul lies between a kind of immortality
And death, approached by daily dying.
Our love is like the angels', our strength as sparrows';
Our life is lived in an earth better than man,
Yet falling short of the soul's vision and desire—
What shall we do?

Our life is lived in an earth where the proofs of God and the soul
Are exactly balanced by disproofs: parallel columns
That say "yes" and "no," item by item. Men must make their choice,
Must form belief according to their hopes, their fears,
Or according to resentment, or courage,
Though resentment and courage are not proof,
Nor is hope, nor fear. What shall we do?
This is earth's triumph.

The Word was too much for the flesh, and when
The Word became the flesh, tragedy and strife were increased,
And earth's idiocy flourished like thistles
Blown everywhere by Satanic breath from the Mount of Olives,
Seeking to make man's predicament harder.
The doctrine was called "love," but when examined
It was found that God would avenge his elect;
That God would repay by being ashamed of those
Who were ashamed of him, that whoever denied God
God would deny—an eye for an eye, a tooth for a tooth, as of old.
The whole of it was fear, produced by curses and threats,
And a pandemic of fear ensued.

It was seen that the Prince of Peace carried a sword,
And at last his followers were sent forth, not without purse or scrip
But with purses and scrip, and with arrows wherewith to enforce tribute.
Nothing was changed from the most ancient days.
And what was the salvation of the world, when the doctrine
Contained bad seed, even if it also contained good seed?
Seeing that, as always, the good seed and the bad seed
Had equal power of propagation, seeing that there was the birth
of the amphisbaenic, the dove and the serpent?
His yoke was heralded as easy,
Yet everyone had to bear his own cross as of old,
And there was no rest.

Seed scattered in stony ground did not sprout, and a good tree
Brought forth good fruit at times, as of old.
Above all this the father was divided from the son, and the mother
Was turned against the daughter, and hate arose
Because dust was shaken from feet by the gates
Of rejecting cities. Lies multiplied in the earth;
The eggs of maggots were laid in the sores of men,
Which hatched into worms that devoured. They were lies,
They were illusions, they were the old contradictions
Of opposed truth and falsehood, but multiplied,
Bringing poison into every hour, and complete insanity at last.
There has been no peace on earth since the angels shouted
"Glory to God in the highest, peace, good will toward men."
There has been no peace, no good will.
There has been strife, there has been hate,
There has been struggle for power, there has been despotism.
There has been war, and with war these things came to pass:
The carpenter's son was worse off than the foxes,
Which have holes for shelter, while he had no place to lay his head.
The fisherman was a beggar, and created a breed
Of mendicants, fanatics. A vast mythology arose
Of angels and devils, supplanting the nymphs and fauns,
Supplanting the profound and beautiful mythology of Athens
Which contains more wisdom, more interpretation of man and earth,
Than all the bibles of the world.

But at last the pope, viceregent of the carpenter's son,
Successor of that fisherman, carrying the keys of heaven,
Commenced to live in a palace and sleep on down, and drink wine,

Not gall, not vinegar mixed with myrrh.
He commenced to lived like the Roman emperors, and to rule an enclave
Which in turn controlled and taxed the world.
He commenced to live in a palace guarded by soldiers
And policemen, waited upon by ambassadors and servants,
And sending ambassadors to states and kingdoms
To bend sovereignties to his will. And kings crawled to him in penitence.
Being afraid of hell, the work of fear was afoot.
He made the whole world his kingdom, though his master proclaimed
That his kingdom was not of this world.
Clothed in purple and fine linen embroidered in gold,
He took account of the world's affairs and waged wars,
Like the Thirty Years War, which was about the Eucharist.
The other cheek was not turned; evil was resisted.
From the beginning he strangled the liberty of hungry peoples,
And choked the life of Spain and Italy
While at the same time praying for peace. And still he prays for peace:
"Give peace, O Lord," he prays. "Give peace in these days," he prays,
"For there is none other that fighteth for us, but only thou, O Lord."
God is love, but god is a warrior, a killer.
"Let there be peace in thy strength, O Lord,
And plenty in thy strong person." This means peace
When every knee is bent, and for the rest
When the battlefield is silent and the vultures are gorged.

When the pirate Sir Francis Drake
Is kneeling at prayer; when France, the art dealer,
Fondles its treasures offered for sale and sends money to Rome;
When America, the business man trying to understand culture,
Attends to business and forgets its faith, its dreams;
When Russia, a back-hall that stinks, stinks again of monarchy;
When Germany, the metaphysician, forgets world commerce;
When Japan, the rat, having crawled the hawser-ropes of pirate ships,
Is breeding in the granaries of China and is gorged and drowsy;
When China is gutted, and forgets Confucius and Lao-tze,
And vermin breed amid the crumbled marbles of T'ien T'an,
The great altar of heaven, and vultures roost on the roofs
And in niches above the arches of Pailou—
That is peace, that is plenty, that is the good end of war.
That is the will of God done in heaven as it is on earth.
That is the triumph of earth.

O beautiful, most beautiful, most insane earth,
This is your triumph!
O beloved earth, loved as a man loves the breasts of a harlot,
Loved as a man loves a woman who has lost her mind
But whose laughter is still music, whose eyes still mirror miracles,
Whose loins still give madness—but whose words tangle,
Whose utterance is idiocy, and with whom continued union
Is torture, is danger.

O blue heaven of white clouds,
And you the stars, numberless in the measureless sky,
Seen from the darkness of the cistern, through the door of the cistern,
It is you that divide our thought; and when we weary of the daily ebb and
    flow
Of human folly, always like senseless and aimless waves;
When symbols are around us and reveal a whole that we cannot see;
When we doubt that our visions and intimations
Are responses to a reality, and the whispering of leaves
Brings no peace against the restlessness of earth;
When the man-god is seen as one who brought death into the world
And all our fear; then we look to you, O stars, to be healed of madness.
And while confessing that life is evil, through you we affirm again that
    life is sweet,
Life is sweet as a bitter drug that turns sweet on the tongue.
For somewhere, somehow, there is faith in us
That earth is constant to law, that the stars are sure;
And though we are slain we accept the cistern,
We accept it as a sacred temple
From which to view waters, mountains, and stars,
And whatever beauty heavenly designs
Have made the object of adoration.

We look up, seeing the stars which look down on us who die,
And affirm that it is good and natural to die
In spite of resistance that rises of itself against death;
In spite of something in us that says
That death is the climax of earth's absurdity,
The summation of the triumph of earth.
And we console ourselves with fields and hills,
With meadows rimmed with white clouds,
With rivers and mountains, and pastures of cattle,
And with sheep by the flags of fresh water.

We thus console ourselves, we the sons of Sisyphus
Who forever roll the stone up the steep
And forever see it roll down again, until it catches and crushes us.
We, the sons of Prometheus, endure the chains and bolts,
Hoping against the shouts of those who brought the undying worm to
        earth,
Hoping to the last against the triumph of earth.

For hate cannot wholly destroy our love;
Fear and doubt cannot wholly destroy our belief.
As there is rock below the quicksands and the swamps,
Beneath the absurdity of this our earth-life
We feel the rock of eternal truth,
Eternal law.
The idiocies, ills, woes of earth
Seem at last as the annual weeds which come and go,
And leave the oak forests standing.

*March 21, 1940.*

(privately printed pamphlet, with a prefacing title-page; no publisher's imprint)

## THE LOTUS IN ILLINOIS

Many summers and winters had come and gone,
Then suddenly the empire was wrecked
When the imperial army met the barbarian foe.
In Yu Chow, An Lu-Shan was stationed
With his star-gleaming legions, there where King Chao
Built his gold pagoda in the days of Tao and peace
And visions.
An Lu-Shan was defeated.
Then passed the jeweled bamboo flute
And pipes of gold. What remained?
The lotus bloomed, and spread its leaves like blue smoke;
Still there were crows by the city wall;
Still there were white clouds over the mountains of Chu,
Though the Ku-Su palace was in ruins,
And the capital of Yueh in ruins.

    \*    \*    \*    \*    \*

All along the rivers and lakes of Illinois
The lotus is now blooming, making earth appear
As yellow as the moon.
From Peoria to Havana, from Havana to Grafton,
Illinois has become a lotus land.
Centuries before, it was a lotus land
When the Indians called the lotus Chinquapin.
And in centuries to come, the lotus will bloom
Up and down the water-courses of Illinois,
Whatever happens to armies, to cities,
To empires, and the ambitions of conquerors—
As now the lotus does not note
The absence of Marquette, La Salle,
Tecumseh, or Black Hawk.

The lotus will never cease to bloom,
The clouds will never cease to sail,
The crows will always fly
Over Starved Rock and the hills of Bernadotte.

    July 29 1941

        (from the author's typescript as reproduced in Hardin W. Masters' book *Edgar Lee Masters: A Centenary Memoir-Anthology.* A.S. Barnes and Co., for The Poetry Society of America, 1972)

# THE BRIDGE

Some slender wires, that make the iron rope
Whereby the massive river bridge is swung,
May rust and part; but yet the bridge will cope
With gravitation and stand where it was hung—
For wires sundered can anew be placed
Or woven again, while traffic still proceeds.
So is it with the heartstrings, being braced
By time with thought and love and gracious deeds.
How can the rope itself break down and part
Which with long-loving artistry was made?
Strands of strong memory hold fast the heart
And make a cable nothing can abrade:
For years of love and living are woven wires,
Compacted of devotions and desires.

(*Good Housekeeping,* February 1942)

# THIS BLOODY AGE

The world is bloody with another birth,
Or dying maybe of a bad miscarriage.
Each quarter of a century, this earth
Pays bitterly for some unfitting marriage.
News of great slaughter, comments on the war,
The radio blabs, if I but turn it on.
I listen, wearied; wonder; and abhor
This idiocy, and wish it to be gone.
I do not sleep for thinking. I arise
Unrested, and take up a listless task;
I reel up from my bed and bathe my eyes,
Which seem half blinded by a netted mask.
What is to do? I think about the dead,
The friends I knew, the long-gone relatives;
Then of myself, who have inherited
This woe too late in life for one who lives—
Strongly, as in my youth—
Still baffled, still in search of truth.

    February 12 1942.


        (previously unpublished)

## AN ILLINOIS SCENE

Not rocks, not hills, not pines, not crystal streams
Rippling in music down a mountainside—
But willows, horse-mint, stunted oaks for dreams,
And mud-banks where the sluggish creek has dried,
And the prairie underneath a glowing sun:
All peaceful and familiar, dear to me.
Here sing the sun birds, here the partridge run,
And here the meadow larks pour melody.

Dear to my heart is all this scene—so plain,
Forbidding, even, to a stranger's eye.
But something in my heart grows into pain,
Striving to fathom this translucent sky.
Here sings the dickcissel, contented bird
That has not wandered from this Illinois
As far east as the Wabash; here is heard
The autumn quail that whistles his meadow joy.

What of world war and triumph in Europe lands
Can obliterate this landscape's charm?
O Nature, guard it with ever faithful hands;
Let nothing change it ever, or bring it harm.
Still nourish the dickcissel, let the weeds
Grow by the muddy creek, let native breeds
Plow here forever on the upland farm.

Aug. 15, 1943

(clipping from unidentified newspaper)

# THE POET'S IMMORTAL FAME

Beginning with Horace and ending with many writers of verse,
I have known men who believed that they had built to themselves
Monuments more lasting than bronze,
Which neither furious winds nor the flight of years
Could destroy, thereby making a part of themselves
A memory which could escape the death-goddess.
They believed that they should grow with time,
Where wild Aufidus thunders
And where Danus, in a parched land,
Should make them famed forever.

But I, having somewhat the eyes of Li Po
Who wandered by the Yangtze
And Yung-ting Lake—
A lover of nature, seeking the solitude of hills,
And the cloud-girt peak of Luh Shan—
See that the Mason County Hills can be leveled
By the winds, and the waters of Spoon River dried
By an act of triumphant nature.
And as for bronze, where is the lettering
On ancient tablets?

If the hills and the river cannot resist remorseless time,
But on the contrary take to themselves later memories,
There may yet be something in the human spirit
More lasting than bronze, and which, having done its work,
Inspires other work, and thereby goes through Protean changes
As eternal as the hills.

(*Asia and the Americas*, December 1944)

# TWO SONNETS

### I.
There is a waste of sundown flags, and through
Their loneliness a stream that moves like grief.
And there are hearts that listen to the brief
Quick aria of the lark that wakes to woo
The dawn, sinking to a bowl of blue
Over a dune as golden as a sheaf
Of summer wheat. And there is Zeneriffe,
And sea-girt forests, caves that hide from view
Air-garmented, rapt presences that thrill
To stand revealed. And there are windless vales
Of apparitions: bluebells, winter green;
And meadow moons, and planets on a hill.
There is this world of Beauty, but it fails
Where love is not, or vanished Love has been!

### II.
There are two deaths, if they be not the same:
One is to look on God; on Beauty one.
No soul has perished seeing God, for none
Has ever gazed into that Face of Flame.
But Beauty may be known of us. Her name
Is also Death, but not oblivion
Through lightning. She is Memory begun,
Who lives to seal our souls up and to maim
With gradual wounds, and make of every wound
An eye which looks on Aprils through the light
Of Aprils gone. She is the Face whose sight
Changes the soul to crystal ere the ground
The body takes, and hearses it in bright
Translucency of pain that makes no sound!

(undated; previously unpublished)

## "Pieces by Puckett":
a sampling of Masters' comic and erotic light verse

## TO AN ORPHAN CLAM

O orphan clam, O orphan clam,
You never seem to give a damn!
You ride upon the summer sea
Indifferent as a thing can be.

You do not grieve about your pa,
Nor eke, I notice, for your ma.
You loll upon the rolling waves
Without regard to parents' graves.

You do not seem to think at all
Of what you lost, or of the pall
That fell upon you when you lost
Your parents in that holocaust:

When they were boiled and afterward
In sizzling skillets of smoking lard
Were fried, to ease the appetite
Of loafers on that fatal night.

You go on careless, without thought
For what misfortune thus was wrought
To social state and education
By death's most awful desolation.

There you swim along the rollers,
And laugh until you show your molars,
Enjoying winds and waves and sun,
And having thus a lot of fun.

O orphan clam, O orphan clam,
I wish to God I was as calm;
I wish that I could sport and laugh
At every lying paragraph.

Thanks for the lesson you have taught,
No matter if it comes to naught.
I'd rather be an orphan clam
Then write the slickest epigram.


(posthumously published in Hardin W. Masters' book *Edgar Lee Masters: A Centenary Memoir-Anthology*. A.S. Barnes and Co., for The Poetry Society of America, 1972)

## COMPENSATION

It isn't very bad to die.
The thing that brings you fears
Is thinking that you won't wake up,
Not in a trillion years.

And yet it may be good to sleep
A sleep whose soundness is
So deep you are not half awake
With a bladder full of piss,
And dreading to get up and make
That extra urine hiss.

(previously unpublished)

## LET THE LOWER LIGHTS BE BURNING

Let the lower lights be burning!
Cast the beam across the pave,
But not so that people turning
Will behold how you behave.
Draw the curtains down if need be;
Do not let the folks look in.
For from shame you will not freed be
If they see you at your sin.

There be lone and ship-wrecked brothers
Who Plain Sewing still commit:
They have all forgot their mothers;
They have fallen in the pit.
They are bold and stand in porches,
Or in holy vestibules,
Playing with their reddened torches,
Growing daily greater fools.

Edwin, turn the lamp up higher!
Let the eyes of passersby
See you sitting by your fire,
Using ointment for your eye—
Never spreading grease or unguent
On that nameless place of yours
Till the smell thereof so pungent
All your sensual power allures,

And you go to seek your fellow
Partner in the sinful act—
With grins both lewd and mellow,
There such business to transact!
Partners in the game Plain Sewing,
It is plain, but what you sow
Is a robe of shame that, growing,
Wrapping you, will bring you low.

Let the lower lights be burning,
But the lights that help a friend,
Not the lights that hide the churning,
Mutual churning, as you bend;
As you hunch and hump and wiggle,
As you glance with furtive eyes,
As you sigh and twist and giggle
Till the instant passion dies.

Let the lower lights be burning!
Jesus calls you to repent!
Would you happiness be earning,
And eternity with him spent?
Well then, listen to my warning:
Quit Plain Sewing right away!
Then you'll wake up in the morning
Ready for a happy day!

(previously unpublished)

## TWO LIMERICKS

A lady named Annabel Lunt
Was possessed of a wonderful cunt.
    She paid all her debts with it,
    Smoked cigarettes with it,
And could make it both whistle and grunt.

    \*

A lady named Evelyn Mott
Put cerise on the lips of her twot;
    And thus she made fucking
    Both fucking and sucking,
And cleaned up a nice little dot.

        (previously unpublished)

## HEAVENLY DISPENSATION

If God decrees, and from the first
Decreed as sin what's called coition,
He would have left some guilty mark
On those who yield to its commission:

Some brand of Cain, some tell-tale change,
Something by way of evidence.
But look! there isn't a single thing:
No scratches, bruises, rips or rents.

What means this, if it doesn't mean
God meant folks should be safe and free,
When nothing happens to the flesh
To show there was adultery?

God helps his children in this wise,
So lock the door and then go to it.
Or fool around—you'll be the same
Whether you do it or don't do it.

(previously unpublished)

# NATURE

I, Lute Puckett, native to Ipava—
Libertarian, student of nature, unreligious but worshipping
All living things, the earth and the sky—
Report certain things hereby to you, and to all of you:
The old, the young, tribads, homos, whores, virgins,
Married women and men, all without distinction
Of race, color, sex habits, or church affiliations.
Listen to me with no blushes: I will not have it.
Don't simper, don't listen and then go back of the barn,
Or into your room, and there resort to self-pollination.
Soberly, and with good sense, listen to my dithyrambs
And be saved thereby.
I will report to you, out of Nature, one story
And only one.
There is nothing else, no matter what your pastor says,
Or Sunday school superintendent,
Or any other person, whether bastard or legitimate.

I have studied algae, blue, green and brown;
I have looked into the fungi of all kinds,
Into slime molds and various bacilli;
Into mildews, liverworts, and mosses;
Into ferns and horsetails;
Into trees: the pine, fir, spruce, hemlock, yew,
The cedar, cypress, redwood, larch, juniper,
The willows, walnuts, and hickories,
The apple, pear, plum, and peach tree.
I have studied strawberries and cactus,
The sweet potato vine, the common potato, the tobacco plant,
The mint plant, the squash, pumpkin, cucumber, and melon.
I have studied grasses, wheat, corn, and palms,
The liana that climbs and squeezes a tree like a man squeezes his
    woman.
I have studied the banana, and flowers of all kinds:
The iris, tulip, narcissus, hyacinth,
The rose admired for its passionate purity,
Orchids, and the lily (taken as a symbol of chastity);
And I find all of these, visible and invisible to the naked eye,

Utterly and constantly
Devoted to fucking.

I have studied amoeba, and living things like obelia,
And the volvox, half plant and half animal;
I have studied sponges, hydras and jellyfish,
Corals and sea anemones;
Flat worms, flukes, roundworms and thread worms,
And ridged worms and leeches;
And starfish, sea urchins, snails, whelks, and slugs,
Oysters, clams, mussels and scallops and water fleas.
I have studied the barnacles, weevils, and June bugs,
May flies, dragon flies, and mosquitoes,
White ants, termites, cockroaches, crickets, and grasshoppers,
Lice, butterflies, spiders and moths, ticks and mites,
And the aphis, that has a virgin birth but reverts to Nature.
And I tell you that all of these are busy all the time:
They are fucking from morning till night,
And I have caught every one of them in the act.

I have pondered the life of fishes,
The sea squirt, lamprey, and hag fish,
Sharks, skates, and stingrays, dogfish and sawfish,
The cod, the mackerel, the salmon
(The salmon will travel upstream a hundred miles for a screw),
The herring, tarpon, trout, pickerels, eels.
I have studied mud puppies, hellbenders, salamanders and newts,
Tree frogs, bullfrogs, lizards large and small,
Serpents, turtles, alligators, and whales.
And I am telling you that each and every of these,
Without exception, are habitues of Nature's whore house,
Which is as broad as Earth itself.
These all spend their time at nothing else
But fucking.

And I have studied birds, from the ostrich
All along the way through penguins and herons,
Ducks, flamingoes, terns, and gulls,
Parrots, owls, and wrens, sparrows and crows,
And the dove, selected by Jesus for its innocence
And as a symbol of the Holy Ghost.
And what did I find?

Each and every of these does nothing but sing,
Waltz, flutter, coo, and play antics
Just to attract the female and persuade her
To let it be put in.
This is Nature's answer to the doctrine of sin;
This is what the Father says to the vice squadron
Headed by the Son and the Holy Ghost.

Is it any different with milk giving animals?
I will take my oath before God it is not.
Look at moles and hedgehogs,
Mice, rabbits and rats and squirrels,
Beavers, pigs and camels,
The giraffe, deer and horses
(Consider the stallion jumping the mare and biting her neck in two),
Cattle (who can overlook the bull armed with a red-hot lightning rod
And testes swinging down like bags of wheat?).
Look at elephants hanging together for a week,
And dogs that will stick for hours;
Look at cats, foxes, the lion, the tiger,
Walruses, seals, sea lions, bears, and leopards.
Have you looked at them, now?
Do you follow my argument?
Then you know that there is but one story:
You know that in the mountains, the jungle, the forests,
The uplands, prairies, valleys, meadows, and fields,
Fucking is going on all the time,
Rain or shine, right in the face of the Holy Scriptures,
Jesus, St. Paul, and everybody opposing it.

And lastly, look at the final word of the story:
Look at the lemurs and marmosets,
The howling monkeys, spider monkeys,
The gibbons, orangutans, chimpanzees and gorillas.
Do they do it to each other?
Come now, don't ask foolish questions,
Seeing that I have spread before you
The whole manifest of living things,
All but man....
Yes, and what of him?
Don't be impatient, I will sing his "sex-life," as the *New Republic*
Phrases the matter.

And you will see that he differs no whit
From the bull, the mite, the lecherous wren,
Or the insatiable dove.

Why, comrade, man has been shown the bottomless pit,
And the fangs of the worm that bites forever,
And the pitchforks of devils heated red hot,
And the wrath of Jesus descending in fire from heaven,
And the hot tears of the Virgin Mary
Grieved to the heart that anyone would be low enough
To take a screw for himself;
And showing wrath besides, and making threats to egg on her Son
To send a sinning soul to eternal fire.
Man has been cursed with the Bible,
With churches and preachers,
With laws against fornication, seduction, and whoredom,
With damage suits for breaking maiden heads,
With books, pamphlets, brochures, essays, poems, sermons,
All directed to prove that fucking is wrong;
And warning people against disease;
And calling the young to purity by persuasions
That "sex," as the *New Republic* calls it, is not necessary to health;
That the young can wait until they have been licensed to screw.
And what is the upshot, the grand summation, the end of the matter?
Why simply this: not a single phallus has been tamed into submission,
And not one maidenhead has been saved:
Not a Goddamned one!

  August 23, 1934


  (previously unpublished)

# NOTES TO THE POEMS

### Love's Philosophy

*Heloise*: Probably Abelard's Heloise, as several other poems in *Songs and Sonnets* present the famous lovers in dialogue. If so, Peter Abelard himself is the speaker.

### Eternal Woman

The title is likely a reference to Goethe's phrase, *ewig-weibliche*, "the eternal Feminine," personified as the Goddess figure "Mater Gloriosa" in *Faust*, part II.

*Nereid*: In Greek mythology, a sea-nymph. Typically imagined as beautiful girls, Nereids are known for helpfulness to sailors.

### Ballad of the Traitor's Soul

*Julian:* Likely a reference to Julian the Apostate (331-363), Emperor of Rome (361-363) who rejected Christianity and promoted the traditional Roman pantheon instead.

*a tithe of anise:* Reference to the words of Jesus in Matthew 23:23: "Ye pay tithe of mint and anise and cummin, and have omitted the weightier *matters* of the law, judgment, mercy, and faith...."

### The Sign

*Harmon Whitney:* Speaker of a poem in *Spoon River Anthology*.

## The Gospel of Mark

The speaker of this poem is the apostle Peter, as internal evidence makes clear. Based on the references identified below, the poem's specific setting within the city of Rome can be determined with remarkable specificity: it lies within Regio VII ("Via Lata") of Caesar Augustus' then-recent administrative reforms—a wealthy neighborhood where, as Peter himself explains, outlaw Christians could meet, clandestinely but in relative safety, in the days or weeks between the Great Fire of Rome in 64 CE and Peter's own death by crucifixion (c. 64 CE).

*Campus Martius:* In English, "Field of Mars"; originally an open plain between the city of Rome and the River Tiber where soldiers were mustered every Spring for military actions. By St. Peter's time, a district of temples within the city itself.

*Collus Hortulorum:* Possibly "Hill of the Small Gardens" or "Hill of the Pleasure Gardens." A neighborhood known for landscape gardens (implying considerable personal wealth), on a hill near the Campus Martius.

*Sallust's garden:* Sallust (86-35 BCE) was a Roman historian. Since he was not living at the presumed time of Masters' poem, the reference is just additional scene-setting.

*they make us lamps:* Likely a reference to the tradition beginning with Tacitus that Nero, blaming disruptive Christians for the Great Fire which he himself may have ordered, had a group of them burned alive in front of the Domus Aurea ("House of Gold"), Nero's own palace which was still under construction at the time of his death in 68 CE.

## Tomorrow is my Birthday

William Shakespeare, the speaker of this poem, died on what is traditionally accepted as his 52nd birthday (April 23, 1616). As the poem indicates, he had in fact revised his will a month earlier, on March 25, and his wife Anne was eight years older than he was.

*Ben Jonson; Michael Drayton:* Two of Shakespeare's fellow poets and dramatists in London.

*robe of Nessus:* Poisoned shirt that killed the Greek hero Heracles (Hercules in Roman mythology).

*urtication:* "A burning or pricking sensation suggestive of pricking with nettles" (Oxford English Dictionary); metaphorical, in the present instance.

## Starved Rock

Title refers to a sandstone butte overlooking the south bank of the Illinois River, a geological formation well-known in the region. Its name derives from an 18th c. Native American legend that, during a lengthy battle between the Illini and Pottawatomie tribes, the Illini took refuge atop the butte and eventually died of starvation. A state park, named for and including the site, was established in 1911.

*La Salle:* René-Robert Cavelier, Sieur de La Salle (1643 -1687), French fur trader and explorer. In 1680 he and French military officer Henri de Tonti built Fort Crèvecoeur downriver from the Starved Rock butte. However, a month after construction was completed on Crèvecoeur, the two men decided that Starved Rock itself would make a better site for a fortification; Crèvecoeur was then sacked and destroyed in order to outfit its replacement, Fort St. Louis— itself abandoned by the time of the Illini-Pottawatomie conflict in the following century.

*whose Memnon lips breathe dirges:* Possibly an allusion linking Starved Rock to the Colossi of Memnon, two 60-foot-high statues of Pharaoh Amenhotep III in the necropolis at Thebes.

## O You Sabbatarians

*hydropots:* "Water-drinkers," i.e. abstainers from alcohol.

## Thyamis

Although this poem may be based on the tale of Thyamis and Chariclea from the ancient Greek text *Aethiopica* ("Ethiopian Stories") by Heliodorus of Emesa (3rd or 4thc. CE), Masters has changed some of the important particulars. In Heliodorus' version, Thyamis is the leader of a band of thieves and Chariclea is the captive of another band, from whom he "steals" her. Attacked by yet a third group of thieves, Thyamis—hopelessly in love with Chariclea, and believing he will lose the battle—kills her, although it turns out that he has unknowingly killed a different woman. The trope of the beautiful heroine captured by an outlaw who falls in love with her, but is then forced to kill her (as he thinks), is common in Greek romances of the period.

## Ulysses

*Ogygia:* Island home of Ulysses' paramour, the nymph Calypso.

## Yet Sing Low

*Yee Bow:* Speaker of a poem in *Spoon River Anthology*.

*cue:* Likely a simplification of "queue," 18th-19th century term for a man's pigtail or braid at the back of the neck.

## The Tombs of the Governors

*waved the bloody shirt:* Reference to a post-Civil-War political tactic (by both major parties) of invoking the war, or war dead, to incite voters against one's opponent.

*Lambert Hutchins:* Speaker of a poem in *Spoon River Anthology*.

*the world made safe for democracy:* An allusion to Woodrow Wilson's 1917 speech to Congress, requesting a declaration of war against Germany because "the world must be made safe for democracy." Congress did as Wilson asked, and the United States entered World War I later that year.

## Horace Knight

*chromo:* Popular 19th-20th c. term for the reproduction of a painting by color lithography, with additional hand-retouching by an artist working from the original.

### Roland Farley

The poem is named for a wealthy New York acquaintance of Masters, a blind musician. He and his wife Elsie put the poet up in their Long Island vacation home after his divorce was finalized (Russell, *ELM* 215-217).

### Jack Kelso

According to local tradition, the real-life Kelso—a well-read New Salem fisherman—befriended the young Abraham Lincoln, introducing the future President to the works of Shakespeare and Robert Burns. Masters subsequently wrote a book-length "dramatic poem" about the relationship between Kelso and Lincoln (Russell, *ELM* 255).

### The Corn

*McLean, / Logan, Menard and Fulton, Sangamon:* Counties in Illinois.

### Worlds

*Thermopylae:* A narrow coastal passage between mountains and sea; site of a famous battle in 480 BCE, where heavily outnumbered Greek forces held off invading Persians until a local shepherd revealed an alternate route, by which the Persians were able to mount a rear attack on the Greeks and defeat them.

### Full Moon on the Bowery

*Nelumbian Lotus:* A species of water-lily native to North America (*Nelumbo lutea*).

*Hua Hsien:* Currently transliterated as "Huāshén": a Taoist flower goddess, sometimes referred to as the "Goddess of 100 Flowers."

*Hangchou:* Currently transliterated as "Hangzhou." In the poem, a reference to Hangzhou Bay on the East China Sea, or the bayside city of the same name.

## The Death of Hip Lung

*nephrite:* A form of jade, white to light yellow in color. Since the name refers to supposed kidney-healing properties of the stone, perhaps Hip Lung's choice of the vase in question provides a hint as to his fatal illness.

## Invisible Landscapes

*terraqueous:* "Living in land and water… extending over land and water, as a journey" (OED).

*La Salle, / Marquette and Joliet:* See notes to "Starved Rock" and "The Lotus in Illinois."

## Hymn to the Earth

*menstrums:* Alternate spelling (and plural) of "menstruum," referring to menstrual discharge. Masters, however, may be alluding more specifically to the word's usage in medieval alchemy, where "the base metal undergoing transmutation into gold was compared to the seed within the womb, undergoing development by the agency of the menstrual blood" (OED).

## The God of the Ailanthus

*ailanthus:* An Asian tree species introduced to North America in the late 18th century. The name in English derives from a Chinese word meaning "tree of heaven" or "tree of the gods."

## Gettysburg

*Pickett:* Confederate General George Pickett (1825-1875), best known for leading "Pickett's Charge," an unsuccessful infantry assault against Union forces at Gettysburg on July 3, 1863. Troops in the charge who got as far as the Union lines were disorganized and quickly repelled; of the 12,500 men under Pickett's command, more than 1,100 died and over 4,000 were wounded.

*Meade stares at Lee and Lee at Meade:* In 1913, a statue of Confederate General Robert E. Lee (1807-1870) and ten soldiers was erected at the Gettysburg National Military Park, some distance from but facing the existing statue of Union General George Meade (1815-1872).

Thothmes: Central Park and The Drive

*Thothmes:* currently rendered "Thutmose." Masters specifically has in mind Pharaoh Thutmose III of Egypt (r. 1479-1425 BCE), on whose orders the obelisk now known as "Cleopatra's Needle" was originally created and erected in the city of Heliopolis. 1,400 years later, Cleopatra VII (69-30 BCE) had the obelisk moved from Heliopolis to Alexandria. Masters deviates from current understanding by suggesting that Caesar Augustus (63 BCE-14CE) ordered this step in the monument's geographical progress, after completing his conquest of Egypt in 30 BCE.

*syenite:* A coarse, light-colored igneous rock found in Egypt.

*Gorringe, U.S.N.:* Lieutenant Commander Henry Honychurch Gorringe, U. S. N. (1841-1885), who transported the obelisk from Egypt to New York City's Central Park in 1880 or 1881.

*this wonder tomb:* Tomb of Ulysses S. Grant (1822-1885), near Central Park. The tomb's identifying architectural features are described in the preceding lines.

*"Let us have peace":* Ulysses S. Grant's Presidential campaign slogan, which is carved over the entryway to his tomb.

*the Half Moon:* Anglicization of *Halve Maen*, name of the ship in which Dutch explorer Hendrik Hudson (c. 1565-c.1611) sailed up the river now bearing his own name.

*our governor newly made:* Likely a reference to the first American Military Governor of the Philippines, Major General Wesley Merritt (1836-1910), installed at the end of the Spanish-American War of 1898 when Spanish island territories in the Pacific were ceded to the United States, according to surrender terms of the Treaty of Paris. Masters was horrified at the time by this annexation, which he considered an act of imperialistic aggression on the part of the American government.

### The Red Cross Nurse

*the rapid Marne, / And Château-Thierry:* These place names and the subsequent descriptions of battle suggest a World War I setting.

### Old Georgie Kirby

*levin:* "Lightning; a flash of lightning" (OED).

### Invulnerable Earth

*the hero of the Hermitage:* Sobriquet of Andrew Jackson (1767-1845), referring both to his actions during the War of 1812 and his mansion in Nashville, Tennessee.

### Spring Lake Village

Title refers to a vacation resort village on the eastern shore of Lake Michigan, where Masters once owned a home. It became an item of contention during Masters' divorce from his first wife, Helen.

### Voice of the Valley

*a poet is asleep / At Skyros:* Skyros is the southernmost island in the Sporades chain off the mainland coast of Greece. English poet Rupert Brooke, a casualty of World War I, is buried there.

### At Midnight in Mytilene

The speaker of this poem is the classical Greek poet Sappho (c630-c570 BCE), who lived in the city of Mytilene (mee-ti-LEE-nee), now capital of the island of Lesbos.

*Leucadian Rock:* According to legend, a high promontory from which unrequited lovers—including Sappho herself, in some sources—threw themselves to commit suicide.

*Neither a navy of ships / Nor a host of soldiers are fairest of things— / The beloved one is the fairest of all:* A reference to the opening lines of Sappho's best-known poem, now designated Fragment 16. Many other allusions to Sappho's work are woven into Masters' poem.

*Hesperus:* Male personification of Venus as the "evening star."

## Medusa

*syenite:* A coarse, light-colored igneous rock found in Egypt.

## There is Labor Whither Thou Goest

*katalysis:* Likely a form of "catalysis." Masters' spelling may be an allusion to the word's original in Greek, meaning "dissolution"—although the context of the poem also suggests its usage in chemistry: i.e., the action of increasing the rate of a chemical change by means of a catalyst (a substance which is not itself changed by the chemical reaction in which it is used).

## In Memory of Alexander Dexter Masters

Title is a reference to the poet's younger brother (1873-1878), whose horrific death from diphtheria haunted Masters to the end of his life.

## Vignettes from Vermont III. Old Mrs. Comstock

*Samantha Allen:* Character in a series of novels by the 19th century humorist and social satirist, Marietta Holley (1836-1926). Her writing, both humorous and serious, focused on prominent social issues of the day: temperance, women's rights, and "the race problem."

## Planting Trees at Tor House

*Tor House:* Stone dwelling on the Carmel, California coast, built and lived in by Robinson Jeffers (1887-1962) and his family.

*George Sterling:* San Francisco poet and playwright (1869-1926), famous in his day for a "Bohemian" lifestyle which may have contributed to the physical deterioration Masters observes in the poem.

*Amphion:* There are several figures with this name in ancient and classical mythology; most likely Masters is referring to the one who, with his brother Zethus, built the city of Thebes in Greece.

## Not to See Sandridge Again

*The Sangamon:* A river in downstate Illinois.

## Spoon River Revisited

*Editor Whedon:* Speaker of a poem in *Spoon River Anthology*. His self-confession includes the lines

> To scratch dirt over scandal for money,
> And exhume it to the winds for revenge,
> Or to sell papers....
> Then to lie here close by the river over the place
> Where the sewage flows from the village....

*Penniwit the artist:* Speaker of a poem in *Spoon River Anthology*.

## Clarence Darrow

Probably the best-known trial attorney of the 20th century, Darrow (1857-1938) saved child-murderers Leopold and Loeb from hanging in 1924, and defended high-school science teacher John T. Scopes (1900-1970) against the crime of teaching Darwinian evolution in the public schools of Dayton, Tennessee (1925). In 1903, Darrow and Masters formed their own law firm in Chicago. Never a happy business partnership, it was dissolved by Masters in 1911. Darrow subsequently represented Masters' first wife in their 1920-23 divorce proceedings, a fact which makes Masters' good-humored, sympathetic character portrayal in 1922 all the more large-hearted... or self-serving.

## The Return

This group of 14 sonnets was culled by Masters from a much larger sequence documenting his own forced "return" from his girlfriend Lillian Wilson to his first wife, Helen, in 1922 (Russell, *ELM*, 194). Nationally famous as the author of *Spoon River Anthology*, his personal life was indeed the stuff of Chicago newspaper stories at the time.

### Hymn to the Unknown God

*Ikhnaton:* Now transliterated as "Akhenaten"; Egyptian Pharaoh (r. 14th c. BCE), known for his ultimately unsuccessful attempt to replace traditional Egyptian polytheism with worship focused solely on the sun god Aten.

*Amarna:* Site of the capital city established by Ikhnaton (Akhenaten). Constructed c. 1446 BCE, it was abandoned soon after his death in c. 1332 BCE.

*Cleanthes:* (c.330-c.230 BCE); Greek philosopher of the Stoic school, whose most famous work is the surviving fragment of his "Hymn to Zeus."

*Rabia:* The single name is just common enough in Islamic culture to suggest several possibilities; most likely Masters has in mind the female Sufi mystic Rābiʿa al-ʿAdawiyya al-Qaysiyya (c.714 - 801 CE), known in the west as "Rabia of Basra."

### End of August

*Salpinx:* Musical instrument with military associations from ancient Greece; a trumpet made of bronze in a straight tube.

*Erebus:* Primordial god of darkness in Greek mythology; offspring of Chaos and sibling of Nyx, goddess of the night, with whom he incestuously fathered several other deities, including the Hesperides, "Daughters of the Evening."

## Li Po

*Li Po:* Currently transliterated as "Li Bo" or "Li Bai." Chinese poet (701-762), whose work is known for its focus on places he visited, friends he enjoyed spending time with, and current events—all three of which are reflected in Masters' poem.

## Amphimixis

Title is a specialized term from biology, referring to "the union of the germ plasm of two individuals in sexual reproduction" (Webster's, 1934). Having extracted the word from its original scientific context, Masters here uses it as a synonym for heterosexual intercourse, whose ubiquity is celebrated in the poem. See "Lute Puckett"'s poem "Nature" for a humorous take on what is essentially the same theme.

*hyphae:* Individual threadlike filaments forming the mycelium or "body" of any fungus, including mold. Mold can produce spores sexually and asexually, both being carried on their hyphae. Sexual spores can be held within the hyphae for several months awaiting conditions suitable to gestation.

*Ulothrix:* A kind of green algae which reproduces both sexually and asexually.

## Hymn to the Universes

Masters' references to the age of both the earth and the universe reflect scientific estimates current at the time of the poem's publication in 1938. Since that information is not essential to the point of the stanza in which it appears, I suspect he was simply indulging his lifelong antagonism toward American fundamentalist Christianity.

## On Seeing *Tannhäuser*

Title refers to the opera by Wagner, whose subject is the conflict between the sensual and the sacred.

The Triumph of Earth

*T'ien T'an:* Currently transliterated as Tiāntàn: the great Temple of Heaven in Beijing.

*Pailou:* Currently transliterated as "paifang"; a type of gate. Masters appears to be using it as a place name, but no cities in China bearing it have the kind of significance attributable to the "Pailou" of the poem. The Lotus in Illinois

*Yu Chow:* Now the You Prefecture, in northern China.

*An Lu-Shan:* Currently transliterated as An Lushan (703-757); Tang Dynasty general and leader of the rebellion that bears his name. His biological parentage is uncertain, but likely non-Chinese or "barbarian"; his name is possibly a Chinese rendering of the Gökturk "Aluoshan." Rivalry with fellow generals and disagreements about subordinate personnel eventually led to his break with the ruling Tang government. Subsequently he declared himself emperor of a new dynasty (the Yan), triggering years of war and political chaos before finally being put down in 763.

*then passed the jeweled bamboo flute:* Here, "passed" is used in the sense of passing out of use, memory, and/or existence.

*the Ku-Su palace was in ruins:* Likely a reference to Li Bo's poem on this subject. Like Masters, Li Bo juxtaposes the destruction and carnage of war with the gradual return of (non-human) life, but the Chinese poem is more of a lament for the former whereas Masters' celebrates the latter.

*Yueh:* Possibly the ancient Yue Kingdom, known to the Chinese as "Eastern Barbarians."

*mountains of Chu:* Chu was another ancient kingdom, allied with the Yue.

*Chinquapin:* Corruption of the Native American word first reported in English as "chechinquamin" by Captain John Smith in 1624. "Water-chinquapin" is an alternate name for the American lotus (*Nelumbo lutea*). See also the notes to "Full Moon over the Bowery."

*Marquette:* Jacques Marquette (1637-1675), French-Canadian Jesuit priest and explorer, who founded the mission settlement of Sault Ste. Marie on what is now the St. Mary's River in present-day Michigan, as part of his effort to win converts to Roman Catholicism among the region's indigenous people. With Louis Joliet, he also explored and mapped the upper Mississippi River valley.

*La Salle:* See note for the poem "Starved Rock." In addition to his activities in Illinois, René-Robert Cavelier, Sieur de La Salle in 1682 led an expedition by canoe from the Illinois River down the Mississippi to the Gulf of Mexico, claiming the entire Mississippi River basin as a possession of France.

*Tecumseh:* Shawnee chieftain and diplomat (1768-1813), noted for his resistance efforts against the expansion of white settlements into indigenous lands of the Great Lakes region. He was instrumental in organizing an inter-tribal confederation whose several thousand Native warriors were allied with British forces against the United States in the War of 1812, during which Tecumseh himself was killed.

*Black Hawk:* Warrior of the Sac (or Sauk) tribe (1767-1838), whose lands were located in the area around what is now Green Bay, Wisconsin. He fought against US forces in the War of 1812, hoping to reclaim Sauk territory from white settlers, and again in the 1832 Black Hawk War against settlers in Illinois and Wisconsin.

## This Bloody Age

*News of great slaughter, comments on the war:* In addition to reports on war efforts in the Pacific and in Europe, Masters—then in his seventies and living at the famously shabby-genteel Chelsea Hotel in New York City—would certainly have heard about German submarine attacks on American ships close to shore. Germans were also widely believed to have been behind the sinking of the *SS Normandie* in New York Harbor on February 9, 1942 (three days before the date of Masters' typescript). The *Normandie*, a French ocean liner, had been seized by US authorities a few months earlier, renamed the *Lafayette*, and was being refitted as a troop ship when it caught fire and capsized.

An Illinois Scene

*dickcissel:* Other than its odd name, there is nothing particularly significant about this small prairie bird—which may indeed be Masters' point in choosing it.


The Poet's Immortal Fame

*Aufidus:* Ancient name for the Ofanto river in southern Italy, arising on the Irpinia Plateau (elevation 2,346 feet) and known for torrential floods during heavy Autumn and Winter rains.

*Danus:* Masters' usage suggests a river name—possibly the Danube, the Dnieper, or the Don, all thought to be etymologically related to Danu, ancient Indo-European water-goddess.


Two Sonnets

*Zeneriffe:* In Masters' typed manuscript, capital "Z" and capital "T" are superimposed as a strikeover, making it impossible to tell which was the final intention. "Zeneriffe" appears to be a 19th century German-language rendering of "Tenerife," the largest of the Canary Islands, themselves a Spanish territory off the west coast of Africa. However, "Zeneriffe" also appears in some Spanish-language references to the island. On the basis of the foregoing (and admittedly sparse) information, I have chosen the more unfamiliar spelling as more interesting and cautiously suggest the island of Tenerife as Masters' intended reference.


Let the Lower Lights be Burning

*Edwin:* Possibly a reference to Masters' lifelong friend, Edwin Parsons Reese of Lewistown, Illinois. In his later years, Masters liked to write obscene letters to Reese, signing himself "Lucius Atherton" in reference to the speaker of a *Spoon River* poem (Hallwas 77). See also the introduction to this book.

*Plain Sewing:* While the context might at first suggest a euphemism for masturbation, or mutual masturbation between two men, other

Puckett pieces make it plain that homosexual anal intercourse is the intended meaning.

## Two Limericks

*cerise:* Popular color for women's lipstick in the 1930's-40's, possibly with connotations of Hollywood glamour.

## Nature

In many respects, this poem is a pendant for Masters' presumably more serious poem on the same subject, "Amphimixis."

*Ipava:* Then as now, a tiny village in Fulton County, Illinois.

*New Republic:* American magazine focusing on cultural and political commentary. At the time the poem was written (1934), it was associated with "scientism," an uncritical application of science or the scientific method to matters outside the actual purview of scientific study. The speaker Lute Puckett's references to it are a satirical commentary on this pseudo-intellectual fad.

www.ingramcontent.com/pod-product-compliance
Lightning Source LLC
Chambersburg PA
CBHW071956110526
44592CB00012B/1104